Sparks (40-15159) 11-1-63

OSWALD GARRISON VILLARD,

Liberal of the 1920's

Men and Movements Series

Oswald Garrison Villard,

LIBERAL OF THE 1920'S

D. Joy Humes

SYRACUSE UNIVERSITY PRESS

1960

Library of Congress Catalog Card: 60–15159

COPYRIGHT © 1960, SYRACUSE UNIVERSITY PRESS

MANUFACTURED IN THE UNITED STATES OF AMERICA
BY THE VAIL-BALLOU PRESS, INC., BINGHAMTON, NEW YORK

To Marjorie Dilley

TEACHER—SCHOLAR—LIBERAL

Preface

AMERICAN LIBERALISM HAS generally been regarded as erratic and unsystematic in its development, and essentially fluid and frequently elusive in its doctrine. As its lack of continuity and consistency are generally accepted, so too is there general agreement that the years 1918–32 covered one of its periodic declines.

Yet it would seem to the more sympathetic observer that there is a semblance of continuity to American liberalism and some consistency in its content. This, after all, is what is implied in the commonly used term "the American liberal tradition."

The pages which follow undertake to demonstrate that the American liberal movement of the current century has lacked neither continuity nor consistency. Close study of the 1918–32 period establishes that liberalism was not in total eclipse during the period; that it was energetically and courageously expounded and defended if only by a handful of men, of whom Oswald Garrison Villard was one; and that the liberalism of this period was a connecting link or bridge between the more articulate liberal programs which preceded and followed it, namely, progressivism and the New Freedom on the one hand and on the other the New Deal.

The method of approach used herein rests on the assumption that a political philosophy in the abstract is incomplete. Its concrete manifestations become clearer through an analysis of some historic figure who attempted to put the theory into practice. The person chosen to represent liberalism in the twenties for the purpose of this study is Oswald Garrison Villard. The liberal faith and liberal crusade were part and parcel of Villard's life. He lavished time and energy in a host of ways and through scores of organizations on the multitude of causes to which he was devoted. Yet no studied attempt has previously been made to place him squarely in the stream of American political liberalism.

Villard's career falls neatly within the scope of a study on recent American liberalism. It began in 1896 with his service on the *Philadelphia Press* and was continued from 1897 to 1918 on the *New York Evening Post*, service which spanned the Square Deal of Theodore Roosevelt, the Progressive movement, and the New Freedom. In 1918 Villard assumed editorship of the *Nation* and did not relinquish it until 1932—the year which marked the advent of the New Deal. Thus his years of active ownership and editorship of the *Nation* coincide exactly with that period of American liberalism generally characterized as in eclipse. These were his most influential years—those in which he made his greatest contribution to the American liberal tradition and earned his reputation as a "fighting liberal."

That which follows is not a biography, although biographical details are utilized to illustrate Villard's philosophy and activities on behalf of liberalism. Neither is this book intended as a history of the period but rather as a study of some of the principal strands of American liberalism in a period of cynicism, disillusionment, and reaction. As such, it cannot avoid history, for political theory does not and should not develop external to the realities of the world with which it deals.

I am indebted to a number of persons who have contributed to this study by providing access to correspondence, records, and personal information about Oswald Garrison Villard, or by otherwise aiding in the research. Sincere appreciation is accorded to Villard's sons, Henry Hilgard Villard and Oswald Garrison Villard, Jr.; to Burton K. Wheeler; to Professors P. R. Coleman-Norton of Princeton University and Russell Nye of Michigan State College; to George E. Belknap, university editor, University of Oregon; to Frank A. Parsons, director of publicity, Washington and Lee University; to Mr. Damon Buell; to Mrs. Lewis Dayton; to the *New York Times Book Review;* to Mr. Philip Slomovitz, editor-publisher of the *Detroit Jewish News;* and to Dr. Volkmar von Zuehlsdorff of the Munich weekly *Die Zeit.*

For kind and resourceful support, the Library Staff of Syracuse University deserves my heartfelt thanks, as does Miss Helen Wurthman of the New York State Library. The capable and expert assistance of Miss Katharine E. Brand, Head of the Recent Manuscripts Section of the Library of Congress, and Miss Carolyn E. Jakeman of the Houghton Library, Harvard University, deserves special note and acknowledgment.

Mr. Konrad C. Mueller, with courtesy and generosity, shared with the author the Villard manuscripts at Harvard, on which he had prior claim because of his projected biography of Villard. His contribution to this study is, therefore, beyond assessment.

I wish also to note my obligation to Syracuse University

for a fellowship grant which made the research for this volume possible and to President Louis Jefferson Long of Wells College for kind and willing support.

I owe an intangible debt to Dr. Lucia Burk Kinnaird, formerly of the University of California and now of Oakland Junior College, for kindling what was a mere spark of interest in public affairs. It was a passing remark of Professor Dwight Waldo of the University of California which roused my interest in Villard, and to him, therefore, my debt is incalculable. To Professor Mary Elizabeth Bohannon of Wells College, I am grateful for continued encouragement and moral support.

My greatest personal debt is to Dr. Marguerite J. Fisher of Syracuse University. To her I offer my special appreciation and most profound gratitude.

D. JOY HUMES

Wells College
June, 1960

Acknowledgments

THE AUTHOR is grateful to the following publishers for permission to make quotations from their publications: to the University of Chicago Press for quotations from "Democracy, The New Conservatism, and the Liberal Tradition in America," by Stuart Gerry Brown, in *Ethics*, 1955; to the Columbia University Press for quotations from *The Progressive Movement of 1924*, by Kenneth MacKay, copyright 1947; to Harcourt, Brace & Co., Inc. for quotations from *The Liberal Tradition in America*, by Louis Hartz, copyright 1955, and for quotations from *Fighting Years: Memoirs of a Liberal Editor*, by Oswald Garrison Villard, copyright 1939; to Longmans, Green & Co., Inc. for quotations from *Borah of Idaho*, by Claudius Johnson, copyright 1936; to Doubleday & Company, Inc. for quotations from *The State Papers and Other Public Papers of Herbert Hoover*, edited by William S. Myers, copyright 1934; to the *Nation* for a quotation from "Oswald Garrison Villard," by Freda Kirchwey, copyright 1949, and for its generous permission to quote freely and liberally from its pages; to the *Reporter* for quotations from letters to the editor by Russell Kirk and William C. Brady, copyright 1955; to the University of Utah for the quotation from "The New Deal: The Progressive Tradition," by Rexford Tugwell, in *Western Political Quarterly*, copyright 1950; and to the *Yale Review* for the quotations from "Toward an American Conservatism," by Clinton Rossiter, copyright 1955.

Contents

OSWALD GARRISON VILLARD,

Liberal of the 1920's

CHAPTER I

Forging of a Liberal

IT HAS BEEN said of Oswald Garrison Villard that he was given a legacy compounded of New England abolitionism, the German Revolution of 1848, and Northern Pacific Railroad shares. To this might appropriately be added that printer's ink flowed in his veins. It would seem almost inevitable that Oswald Garrison Villard should have become both a newspaperman and a liberal crusader, for he inherited a family background unique for its richness in those pursuits, on the maternal as well as the paternal side.

Villard's father, Heinrich Hilgard, was only thirteen when he took his stand on the German Revolution of 1848. He chose to support his uncle, Friedrich Hilgard, the head of the provisional revolutionary government of Bavaria, rather than his father, a judge, who had remained loyal to the throne. The subsequent collapse of the revolution with its accompanying reaction, and the parental ire which pursued him, ultimately led to Heinrich Hilgard's adoption of the name Henry Villard and his flight to America in 1853. Eighteen years of age, unable to speak English, and with only twenty borrowed dollars to his name, Henry Villard proceeded to make for himself a fortune and a place in American history. He began as a newspaperman, first reporting the Lincoln-Douglas debates in German for the New

York *Staatszeitung*. There followed assignments on the *Cincinnati Commercial*, *St. Louis Missouri-Democrat*, *New York Tribune*, and *New York Herald*. Among his assignments were the discovery of gold in Colorado and the Civil War battles at Bull Run, Shiloh, Fredericksburg, Charleston, and Missionary Ridge.

Sent as a war correspondent by the *New York Tribune* to the Austro-German War, Henry Villard arrived after the cease-fire, but remained for two years. It was during a return visit to Germany in 1872 that his son, Oswald, was born on March 13, and Henry became associated with the German stockholders of the California Railroad Company, marking the beginning of his contribution to the history of transportation in America. Asked to become a member of the bondholder's protective committee, he returned to America as its official representative. He later joined a similar committee of the Kansas Pacific Railroad Company. He became manager of these two committees and also of the Oregon Steamship Company. Subsequently he became president of the railroads and a receiver of the steamship company. In 1881 he purchased controlling interest in, and became president of, the Northern Pacific Railroad. It was under his management that the transcontinental line was completed. The Golden Spike ceremony was to stand out vividly in Oswald Villard's memory, for he "saw his father the center of a tremendous celebration in one city and state after another, . . . beheld him ranked in public honor with the then President of the United States, and acclaimed almost as much as the distinguished ex-President and conqueror of the Confederacy, General Grant." [1]

[1] Oswald Garrison Villard, *Fighting Years: Memoirs of a Liberal Editor* (New York: Harcourt, Brace & Co., 1939), p. 46.

It was in 1881 also that Henry Villard, apropos of his continuing interest in journalism, bought the *New York Evening Post* and its weekly supplement, the *Nation*, which was subsequently to become the vociferous instrument of Oswald Garrison Villard's liberalism.

In addition to making newspaper and railroad history, Henry Villard played an important part in the development of electricity in America. In 1893 he purchased the Edison Lamp Company and the Edison Machine Works which became the Edison General Electric Company under his leadership and presidency, and later became the General Electric Company. Villard, along with J. P. Morgan and others, had been subsidizing Edison for some years. Edison reportedly acknowledged that he could never have achieved what he did without the complete faith and aid of Henry Villard, one of the few men to visualize the potentialities of electricity. "In pioneering," said Edison, "you have to have a man with nerves to adopt your ideas. I have found the man. He is Henry Villard." [2] Villard was the first to attempt the application of electricity to railroads. He contracted with Edison to build the first electric railroad in America at Menlo Park, hoping that he could adopt its passenger locomotive for the Northern Pacific. The system which resulted was that which came into use on the New York Central and New Haven roads. Villard is also credited with building the first electrically lighted steamship, the *Columbia*, in 1879.

This, then, was Oswald Garrison Villard's father—youthful rebel and republican, war correspondent and newspaper

[2] Quoted in William Adams Simonds, *Edison, His Life, His Work, His Genius* (New York: Blue Ribbon Books, Inc., 1940), p. 266.

owner, railroad financier and promoter of the practical application of electricity.

Next to his father, Villard's greatest heritage was perhaps
from his maternal grandfather, William Lloyd Garrison, to
whom has been attributed the "puritan pull" in Villard's
blood. Surely the fact that his Grandfather Garrison was
the Great Liberator had some causal relationship to the
fact that Oswald Villard became one of the founders of the
National Association for the Advancement of Colored People. It has been said of William Lloyd Garrison that he
was taught by a pious mother to see moral implications in
all things. He could conceive of slavery, for example, only
as a moral issue, a national sin. His intransigence in the
matter led to a split among the antislaveryites—a split along
the lines of whether abolition was a moral or a political
problem and consequently a difference over the methods
and tactics to be adopted by the abolitionists. Wendell
Phillips Garrison, son of the Great Liberator and uncle of
Oswald, in speaking of the poetry his father had written
from the time he was sixteen, noted that nearly every piece
bore the stamp of the moralist. It is not too surprising, then,
to hear that Oswald Villard, finding himself faced with
losing an argument on political grounds, would resort to
making a moral issue of the problem involved or that he was
quick to find moral implications in the other man's point
of view. A close associate of Villard on the *Nation* has
written of him that "he would never have disputed another
man's right to disagree with him about peace or racial equality or free trade; but it was hard to persuade him that such
contrary views were sincerely held or honestly advocated.

To him they were simply wrong, and to harbor wrong opinion was at least circumstantial evidence of evil motives." [3] Villard himself called attention to this characteristic: "I have never been able to work happily with men or women who are incapable of hot indignation at something or other—whether small or big, whether it stirred me personally or not, if only it was something. To minimize every evil is to my mind to condone it and in time to destroy one's influence." It was Villard's infectious moral indignation that was to inspire his *Nation* staff in the years in which it was molded into the most effective crusading organ of its day.

Recalling that the banner headline of William Garrison's first issue of his antislavery journal, the *Liberator* was "Our country is the World—Our countrymen are all mankind," it seems appropriate for his grandson to have taken a special interest in international affairs and to have added an International Relations Section to his liberal weekly, the *Nation*, at a time when it was not yet fashionable to be "world-minded."

Again recalling the masthead of the *Liberator*, "I am in earnest—I will not equivocate—I will not excuse—I will not retreat a single inch—AND I WILL BE HEARD," one can more readily understand and sympathize with the uncompromising nature of the grandson of that journal's editor when, in a radio address on the eve of relinquishing the editorship of the *Nation*, he said:

It is not, of course, easy to thrust away at the injustice on every hand, nor to seem to be the perpetual caviler. But it is far far worse to be a compromiser; to be a toadier

[3] Freda Kirchwey, "Oswald Garrison Villard," *Nation,* CLXIX (October 8, 1949), 340.

to things as they are; to bow the knee to Baal; to seek only to advance one's own interest and let the devil take the hindmost . . . . Nobody can, I hope, truthfully aver that I ever compromised on a principle, or failed to tell the truth as I saw it.

On another occasion, one on which he admitted that he was taking an uncompromising position on an issue, Villard reiterated the words of his grandfather's good friend, Wendell Phillips, "I must entrench myself upon principle and leave the working out of details to Almighty God."

As his grandfather found it necessary, or at least convenient, to publish his own newspaper to assure that he would be heard, so too did Oswald Villard. Again and again he justified his independent weekly in terms of the need for maintaining a free press and the need for providing a medium through which a minority might be heard. "What," he asked, "is to be the hope for the advocates of new-born and unpopular reforms if they cannot have a press of their own, as the Abolitionists and the founders of the Republican Party set up theirs?"

Villard's personal correspondence abounds with references to his mother, Fanny (Helen Frances) Garrison Villard. Their relationship was an exceptionally close and binding one, and she exerted a tremendous influence on his personal character. Villard might well have been describing his mother's son rather than his mother when he wrote, for example, that like her father before her, she "was incapable of compromise, without being either a bigot or narrowly puritanical . . . . To modify any position she took for reasons of expediency—that was unthinkable; to shift her ground in order to gain a personal advantage, or to avoid unpleasantness, was as impossible for her as for her father." [4]

After her husband's death in 1900, Fanny Garrison Villard took a more active part in the causes to which she had long been devoted—woman suffrage, the Negro problem, and peace. She was president of the Women's Peace Society from 1919 to 1928 and was active in the National Association for the Advancement of Colored People and the Woman Suffrage Association. She made the major address on behalf of the Woman Suffrage Association in Boston on February 23, 1910, when 1,500 women paraded from State House to Ford Hall in pursuance of their cause. One would seem justified in assuming that she influenced her son in his acquiescence to the request of Dr. Anna Shaw, president of the National Woman Suffrage Association, that he form a Men's League for Woman Suffrage which he did with the aid of Professor Max Eastman. Fanny Garrison Villard took justifiable satisfaction in the record made by the men of her family on the woman suffrage movement. "It gives me joy," she once remarked publicly, "to remember that not only my father, William Lloyd Garrison, but also my good German-born husband believed in equal rights for women." [5] It must indeed have given her additional satisfaction at a later date to see her son as he walked down New York's Fifth Avenue in the first woman suffrage parade—one of a handful of men that day who braved both jeers and rotten eggs.

[4] Villard, *Fighting Years*, p. 21.
[5] In Ida H. Harper (ed.), *The History of Woman Suffrage* (New York: National American Woman Suffrage Assn., 1922), V, 244.

Oswald Villard remarked upon his indebtedness to his family background as follows: "These were the 'divergent' strains which made me what I am. These were the parents who gave me every opportunity in life, every benefit that wealth could bestow and forged for me the tools that I used in my effort to mold the public opinion of my time." [6] From this background emerged one who was to carve out a life embracing the roles of college teacher, newspaper reporter, editor, publisher, author of numerous books, businessman, and club man. Out of it grew a man accused of being a spy, traitor, liar, pro-German, the rankest negrophile in America—a man known, on the other hand, as reformer, fighting liberal, liberal crusader, fighter for truth, honor, justice, and fair dealing, a man who feverishly attacked everything he thought was wrong.

Villard's early childhood was divided between New York City and his father's summer estate at Thorwood, Dobbs Ferry. As a youngster he attended New York's private Morse School. In the fall of 1889 he entered Harvard where he had what he described as an undistinguished career, and from which he graduated in 1893. He returned to Harvard after a year of travel in Europe to study for the master's degree in history and to act as assistant to Professor Albert Bushnell Hart in the area of United States history. Villard regarded himself as not really a competent teacher; he records that, while he enjoyed it, he did not find teaching sufficiently stimulating to wish to make a lifetime career of it. To his father, who wanted him to stay in the teaching

[6] Villard, *Fighting Years*, p. 23.

profession, he explained that teaching was out of the stream of everyday events. "It is," he explained, "like sitting in a club window and watching the world go by on the pavement outside." He chose instead to go into journalism, where distinguished service was to merit him an honorary Phi Beta Kappa key from Howard University; an honorary Doctor of Literature degree from both Washington and Lee and Howard Universities; and an honorary Doctor of Laws from both Lafayette College and the University of Oregon.

In addition to an active writing career spanning the years 1896 to 1947, Villard had considerable stature as a businessman. He was president of the Fort Montgomery Iron Company, Garrison Realty Company, and City Club Realty Company and was a director of various banks in New York City. He was owner of the *Nautical Gazette*, a journal of marine news, and he founded *Yachting* magazine.

Villard was an active club man. He was vice president and trustee of the New York City Club for eleven years, president of the Philharmonic Society from 1915 to 1917, and a member of the Harvard, Century, and University Clubs in New York City, as well as the Cosmos Club in Washington, D.C. Needless to say, there were many times when his liberal views conflicted with those of his fellow club members. Villard would profess hurt and puzzlement upon being avoided at luncheon at one of his clubs, seemingly unable to comprehend why his friends should take personally his attacks on Wall Street, tariffs, and trusts. One writer has remarked of Villard in this respect that "if he was given wealth, he was taught to look beyond it. It enabled him to sit with the titans of the day and to despise them; it gave him what the self-made, the greedy, the hangers-on never possessed and could never afford to possess—the sense of their own futility." [7]

Villard's facility for writing was apparently phenomenal. Reminiscing members of the *Nation* staff to this day marvel at the speed with which he wrote editorials. His pen always busy, Villard was the author of many books. Among them are: *The Early History of Wall Street* (1897); *John Brown: A Biography Fifty Years After* (1910); *Germany Embattled* (1915); *Some Newspapers and Newspapermen* (1923); *Prophets True and False* (1928); *The German Phoenix, the Story of the Republic* (1933); *Fighting Years: Memoirs of a Liberal Editor* (1939); *Inside Germany* (1939); *Our Military Chaos: The Truth About Defense* (1939); *The Disappearing Daily* (1944); *Free Trade, Free World* (1947). These titles reflect only a few of Villard's interests—history, journalism, international affairs, and economics.

In addition to writing books and writing for his own *Nation*, Villard contributed to such journals as *Century*, *Scribner's*, *Harper's*, *Forum*, *Christian Century*, and *Progressive*.

Oswald Villard had had only six months experience as a reporter for the *Philadelphia Press* when he presented himself for work on the *New York Evening Post* on May 24, 1897, at the insistence of his father, its owner, and Horace White, then second in charge to the editor, Edwin Godkin. The *Evening Post* was one of New York's oldest and most distinguished newspapers. Founded in 1801, some claim by Alexander Hamilton, it numbered among its distinguished

[7] Alfred Kazin, "America at High Noon," *American Mercury*, XLVII (June, 1939), 241.

editors William Cullen Bryant, Carl Schurz, Edwin L. Godkin, and Horace White. Villard's father had purchased controlling interest in the *Evening Post* in 1881. Upon his father's
death Villard inherited the paper, assumed its presidency,
and shaped its policy until he relinquished it in 1918.

Villard has been credited with having done much through
the *Evening Post* to mold the philosophy of the New Freedom and to guide President Wilson in his first administration. The *Evening Post* warmly supported Wilson in his
gubernatorial campaign of 1912 and has been credited with
influencing the intellectuals to flock to Wilson's support and
in general giving nation-wide impetus to the Wilson boom
for the Presidency.

Villard's views on preparedness and universal military
training and his opposition to American entry into World
War I made him and the *Evening Post* unpopular. Loss of
advertising contracts and subscribers made the financial
situation of the *Evening Post* so precarious that in the summer of 1918 Villard was forced to sell it. He comforted
himself with the thought that he had stayed with it as long
as possible, in his family tradition. "Whatever else may be
said of us," he wrote, "we don't run under fire. I accomplished what I wished to—keeping our great paper from
becoming like all the others, a Hun-hater and suppressor
of news." [8]

On February 1, 1918, Villard had assumed the editorship
of the *Nation*, which, because of its practice of reprinting
Evening Post articles, had become characterized as a kind
of weekly edition of the daily. As a forerunner to the sale

[8] Villard, *Fighting Years*, p. 333.

of the *Evening Post*, Villard, on June 28, 1918, announced
the complete editorial separation of the *Nation* from the
Post. With its editorial independence thus publicly established, and himself lodged as editor, Villard secured full
ownership of the *Nation* for himself at the time he sold the
Evening Post to Thomas W. Lamont.

Villard's direct connection with the *Nation*, begun in
January, 1894 with his first contribution, was to continue
for half a century. From 1900 to 1918 he was editorial writer
and president of the Nation Press, Inc. He was editor and
owner of the *Nation* for fourteen years, from February 1,
1918 to December 31, 1932; publisher and contributing editor from 1933 to 1936; and an editorial associate from 1936
to 1940, at which time he broke with the editorial board over
its nonpacifist policy toward the war in Europe.

The pages which follow are primarily concerned with
the period during which Villard was solely responsible for
the *Nation*'s policy by virtue of being its owner, editor,
and publisher—the years 1918 to 1932. Significantly, the
circulation figures of the weekly jumped in the first two
years of Villard's editorship from 7,200 in 1918 to 38,087
in 1920. While they never exceeded 38,087 under his editorship, they never fell below 24,732. One needs only to compare circulation figures prior to and since Villard's editorship
to gauge his effectiveness with the *Nation*. Under the great
Edwin L. Godkin, the *Nation*'s circulation never exceeded
12,000. Under Villard's immediate successor, Freda Kirchwey, it topped his record circulation in only six of the
twenty-two years of her editorship. In 1959 the *Nation*'s
circulation stood at 26,601, considerably below the 35,409
figure of 1932 when Villard gave up the editorship.

These circulation figures are not large, and their number

alone cannot be taken as a measure of the *Nation*'s influence and consequence under Villard's leadership. Periodical literature does not lend itself readily to measurement of its political influence. Historians have noted, however, that during the period 1918–28 the task of influencing opinion by direct discussion was largely taken over by liberal weeklies such as the *Nation* and the *New Republic*. However difficult it may be to measure quantitatively the influence of Villard's *Nation*, it stands as a voice of American liberalism in the years 1918–32.

Villard gave up control and management of the *Nation* on December 31, 1932, at which time he expressed his hope of continuing to write for it "until Death do us part," but this was not to be. He contributed weekly signed articles until June 31, 1940, when his uncompromising pacifism, maintained steadfastly through three wars, led to a sharp break with his staff over military training and aid to the Allies. Villard had lost the *Evening Post* as a result of his editorial policies in the First World War, and thus the Second World War led to his alienation from the *Nation* forty-seven years after his first contribution appeared in it. *Christian Century* and the *Progressive* then became the primary media for the voicing of Villard's opinions.

In October of 1944, Villard suffered a heart attack in the office of his longtime friend Norman Thomas, and from that time until his death five years later, on October 1, 1949, he was able to do very little writing.

Oswald Garrison Villard may not have been a truly great editor; this, it would seem, is debatable. It should be noted also that he was neither a political theorist nor a philosopher in that he made no attempt to create a complete system of political thought. The fact remains, however, that he was one of the best known political journalists in the United States in the 1918–32 period, and he was one of the few outspoken, crusading liberals of his time. Villard's causes, as will be seen in subsequent pages, embraced most of the great controversies of the first half of the twentieth century, and his record for genuine liberalism has not been surpassed.

A journalist in an era of disillusionment with democracy and of postwar reaction, Villard was an acute observer of the world of which he was a part; he was an interpreter of the political and social scene; and he attempted to correct the political and social evils or abuses of his day. In so doing he did much to define and defend the liberal position of the 1920's.

CHAPTER II

American Liberal Tradition

THE TERM LIBERALISM has acquired two seemingly contradictory meanings. Historically and in the broader sense it refers to that movement which emphasized the abuse of political power and thus was concerned with the individual's freedom from governmental restraint and ecclesiastical tyranny. This movement realized its greatest potential in constitutional democracy standing opposed to autocracy, despotism, and tyranny. It concentrated on securing political freedom and, through free trade and removal of the hindrances to industry left by the survival of feudal regulations, limiting the interference of the state in economic affairs. In this sense it is rightly identified with the rise of democracy and of capitalism as they developed in Britain, France, and the United States in opposition to the feudalism and aristocracy of Europe's past.

There is, however, a stream of thought which may be said to constitute liberalism within liberalism—that *more* liberal element within an already democratic or liberal, as the term is used above, society. Almost a century ago, Walter Bagehot, an exceptionally keen observer of British politics, called attention to the fact that there are always two principal forces operative in politics everywhere—a conservative and an innovating or revolutionary force—and that consequently the political world, whatever may be its boundaries, is divided into two camps: the conservative embodying the inheritance of the past on the right, and the liberal facing the necessity of the present and hopes for the future on the left.

In an America which had no feudal past, historic liberalism became conservatism, a conservatism identified with the defense of the *status quo* which tends to contain liberty within a traditional pattern rather than embrace new acquisitions to liberty. Liberalism, on the other hand, considers the present and the future as well as the past and sponsors innovation and reform. It is a liberalism possible in those societies which, in the words of Lord Balfour, are composed of a people so fundamentally at one that they can safely afford to bicker. To elaborate, it might be noted that while conservatism and liberalism may be contrasted, they are not essentially antithetic. American liberals and conservatives both, for example, are concerned with civil liberties; both would defend our basic political institutions; both desire to preserve economic opportunity. They differ, for the most part, over extensions of liberties, of the consent of the governed, and of economic opportunity and over methods of achieving particular social objectives. The American conservative, fearing political power, tends to view governmental action as dangerous to freedom. The liberal, fearing economic power and surrounded by its growing concentration, seeks refuge in state action.

That tradition in American social history which may be characterized as recent American liberalism, and with which this volume is concerned, dates from about 1865. It is a liberalism which has demanded a positive program of governmental action to achieve certain social, economic, and political ends; one which has embraced social justice as well as the juridical and political institutions which make the liberal state. Thus recent American liberalism may be said to have had its beginnings with the Grangers, Greenbackers, and Populists and to have proceeded through progressivism, the New Freedom, and the New Deal.

It should perhaps be noted here that the conservative-liberal dichotomy in American politics has not always been represented by a strict divergence of the two major political parties. When the principal tenets of the two major parties have tended to coalesce, for example, the liberal elements have been found nurturing themselves either entirely outside both parties, as, for instance, in the Populist or People's Party, or as defections from those parties such as the Progressives of 1912. Whether the liberal element in recent American politics has been found in the Democratic Party or in defections from the Republican Party, or again in third parties, it has been based on the same underlying principles. Both the Square Deal of Republican Theodore Roosevelt and the New Deal of Democrat Franklin D. Roosevelt were sets of ideas concerning various aspects of social organization and governmental policy. These two sets of ideas had something in common which caused them both to be typified as liberal. The crucial question is, "What makes them *characteristically* liberal?" Recent liberalism has after all embraced a variety of so-called causes—civil liberties, national self-determination, free trade, pacifism, and humanitarian reform, to mention only a few. Underlying these causes are certain fundamental principles which constitute the liberal formula and thus shape the rationale for their adoption and consequently for the attachment of the "liberal" label to them.

The isolation, analysis, and synthesis of these principles are vital to a clear understanding of American liberalism and to the study of liberal manifestations in any given period of history. Strangely enough, little attempt has been made by analysts of American liberalism to do so. Too many have been content to write liberalism off as an attitude or a state of mind. Few writers have joined John Dewey in a deliberate attempt to attribute philosophic content, clear-cut or not, to recent American liberalism and to consider it as a conscious and aggressive movement.

Any attempt at such an analysis would need to recognize first and foremost that liberalism is rooted in humanism, a philosophy which sets up as the chief end of human endeavor the happiness, freedom, and progress of all mankind. But American liberalism is highly individualistic. It places the human personality (existence as a self-conscious being) at the center of its system of values. It is devoted to the supreme worth and dignity of the individual man and stands for his fullest and freest development. It insists that the individual maintain his personal freedom, obey his own conscience, and not be content to be a mere item in the multitude. It is this individualistic factor in American liberalism which is responsible for the belief that the most important criterion for measuring the success or failure of social organization and institutions is their effect on the destiny of the individual. The function of the liberal becomes that of translating into political reality those opportunities without which men cannot attain their fullest potential. Individualism in turn embraces several related doctrines, namely rationalism, libertarianism, and humanitarianism.

In its appeal to reason, American liberalism has been an appeal to the reason of the common man rather than to that of a select few. It recognizes that men must live together in organized society and that the society itself helps to shape their destiny. It assumes that men are sufficiently reasonable to meet the necessity of modifying those social institutions which they feel do not operate to the best interests of human welfare. It assumes further that they are reasonable enough to do so without resort to violence, through deliberation rather than reliance on the arbitrary force of governmental authority. Recognizing that political power necessarily exists in any organized society, the American liberal is concerned with both its use and its abuse. Assuming that each individual is rational enough to share in the governmental process, the liberal is concerned with enlarging his opportunity to do so, thus enlarging his opportunity to direct the use to which government is put. His emphasis on the rationality of human beings and human institutions imposes upon the liberal categorical opposition to the exercise of unlimited power.

In its more strictly libertarian aspect, American liberalism has become identified with the defense of individual civil liberties. The American liberal still believes that certain rights are inviolable, not only as means for the realization of other values but as values in themselves. Man is entitled to certain rights by virtue of his capacity for independent thought and action. Thus rights become the legal recognition of the worth of human personality. The American liberal, however, is not content with the mere legal form of individual rights. He has been so insistent on the living substance of such rights that he has been accused of becoming professional in his search for their violation. He recognizes that self-government is meaningless and individualism and rationalism are prostrate without freedom of thought and expression, a free press, and free assembly. It follows naturally that the liberal has been insistent on tolerance and tenacious in his defense of minorities. An ever-present concern is that minorities shall be enabled to become majorities.

The American liberal has extended his concern over civil rights to include protection against abuse by private individuals as well as protection against the encroachment of government. The American liberal would increase the scope of governmental activity in this area. President Truman expressed this point of view when he said that "the extension of civil rights today means not protection of the people against the Government but protection of the people by the Government." [1]

The doctrine of individual rights has undergone for American liberals another extension—one which has created new rights for the individual, new rights which tend to re-enforce the traditional. Historically, humanitarianism and libertarianism have been closely related doctrines. The American liberal would seriously question the value of the individual's right to freedom of thought and expression if that individual were denied, overtly or otherwise, a fair opportunity to a minimum of education. Freedom of the press, the liberal would hold, is meaningless to those unable to read. The liberal contends that those social measures which tend to ameliorate poverty and ignorance operate to enlarge the individual's freedom. The individual becomes free to do

[1] *New York Times*, June 30, 1947, p. 3, col. 1.

and enjoy things unavailable to him if the attainment of certain social conditions are left to his own or private initiative. Thus the liberal conception of liberty is one that embraces every aspect and phase of human life—liberty of thought, of expression, and of cultural opportunity and the belief that such liberty is not to be had without a degree of economic security. The American concept of liberty then has been expanded to include positive as well as negative freedoms—freedom "to" as well as freedom "from." It has been extended to include such new rights as that of security from economic hazards over which the individual has no control, and the right to organize and bargain collectively.

Based on the individualistic premise that a person is entitled to respect simply because he is a living human being, and recognizing that the individual is subject to conditions beyond his control which are the responsibility of society, American liberalism committed itself to the use of governmental power to remedy those evils, environmental and economic, from which the less fortunate classes suffer. To this extent, it is indeed humanitarian.

This, then, is the philosophic content of American liberalism. From a fundamentally humanistic base, it has embodied individualism, rationalism, libertarianism, and humanitarianism. In its practical application of these precepts, American liberalism has appealed, through the government, for collective social action. It has demanded a positive program of governmental action to provide the conditions—economic, political, and other—which would give the common man the opportunity to realize the essential dignity to which he is by nature entitled. It is in its philosophic content and in its method of social engineering that the consistency and continuity of American liberalism is to be found.

While American liberalism may appear historically to have stood for different things at different times, actually it has been its specific, concrete programs or policies which have changed from time to time to meet new challenges. Its underlying values have remained much the same. Consider the concept of liberty which is, after all, basic to historic liberalism. The abstract concept is always valid, but its concrete application is relative to any given situation which contains institutions deemed oppressive or totalitarian.

Historically, then, the task of American liberals has been that of relating liberal values to the solution of contemporary problems. More recent American liberalism may be said to have its inception in movements dealing with the effects of industrialization and the accompanying concentration of wealth. The inequities of the economic system have been the cardinal point of liberal activity from the late 1800's until at least the Second World War.

In addition to, and not totally unrelated to, his preoccupation with economic abuses, has been the liberal's concern for more democratic political institutions. His demand for new means of political control, his absorption with economic problems, and the manner in which he related his liberal values to the solution of those problems may be illustrated in a brief sketch of the evolution of recent American reform movements.

In the latter decades of the nineteenth century, protest against conservative control of the government by both major parties expressed itself in a variety of movements. Twentieth-century American liberalism had its inception in the activities of Grangers, Greenbackers, and Populists.

These agrarian reformers formed the vanguard of twentieth-century liberals. The Grangers, in their pressure for railroad and warehouse regulation in the 1870's, set the stage for the issue of the railroad and the trust questions of the next fifty years.

The Greenbackers, in their attempt to come to grips with falling prices and unemployment, focused attention on the inelasticity characteristic of the financial system and on currency instability. The former was not met squarely until the Federal Reserve Act of 1913, and the latter is still a matter of serious concern.

The Populists, cultivating soil already tilled by the Grangers and Greenbackers, went much farther in their economic program. They not only campaigned for government ownership of railroads, for control of the stock and bond issues of public service corporations, and for free coinage of silver, but for compensation to labor for industrial accidents, for a graduated income tax, and for tariffs for revenue only. The Populists coupled their economic reforms with political reforms. They urged the Australian ballot, corrupt practices legislation, the establishment of primary elections to replace conventions and caucuses, the direct election of United States Senators, the initiative, and the referendum. In short, the Populists were concerned with furthering democracy—political as well as economic. They recognized that the powerful and often corrupt economic interests could better be controlled when the people had assumed more control over their government.

Underlying all of the reform movements of the late 1800's was a common theory—that of individual rights. Implicit in the Granger resolve that the conduct of the railroads be made to serve the public interest was the belief that the individual's right to liberty, equality of opportunity, and the pursuit of happiness was in some way being violated. The Populist protest was a protest against social injustice and violations of the dignity of the human being. The Populists, spiritual descendants of the Grangers, contrasted their traditional idea of America (as the land of opportunity, the land of the self-made man, free from class distinctions and from the power of wealth) with the existing America and found it sadly wanting. The agrarian agitation of the seventies, eighties, and nineties represented a revolt against the power of urban industrial enterprise. It sought to protect the American tradition of individualism and equality against the social and economic forces by which these were threatened. It relied for method upon attaining more democratic political institutions and turning those institutions to the task of control and protection.

However, while the Grangers, Greenbackers, and Populists contributed significantly to the basic legislation and philosophy of government regulation of business, they formed for the most part only vociferous minorities, gathering strength mainly from the rural Midwest and South. It remained for Bryanism to nationalize populism. Bryan touched hands with both the populism of the nineteenth century and the progressivism of the twentieth. In Bryan the unrest of both the rural and urban population began to coalesce. Believing in equal rights for all men and special privileges for none, he advocated bimetallism, a lower tariff, the regulation or destruction of monopoly, an income tax, direct election of United States Senators, and even government ownership of railroads.

It was not, however, until after the turn of the century that liberal reform gained respectability in the eyes of a majority of the people, thereby making the whole movement of significance in American history and tradition. It was in the early years of the century that the conditions of urban life, employment on a large scale, and the power of economic concentration began to be directly felt by a majority of the population. Only then was the liberal movement enabled to become a middle-class movement.

Progressivism virtually swept the country in the first decades of the 1900's. The spade work was done first in single states, then nationally. Reform of the machinery of state governments took the form of acceptance of the direct primary, initiative, referendum, and recall. Women's suffrage, the direct election of United States Senators, and the shorter ballot were also part of the movement to make government more responsive and more responsible to the populace. In terms of legislation to meet social and economic problems, agitation in the states supported industrial safety legislation, workmen's compensation laws, prohibition of child labor, and minimum wage standards.

On the national scene in 1901, Theodore Roosevelt was suggesting more effective regulation of trusts, extension of the powers of the Interstate Commerce Commission, conservation of natural resources, and extension of the Civil Service. Four years later he was paying lip service, at least, to the enforcement of antitrust legislation, currency and banking reform, and federal control of child labor. By 1910, Roosevelt was speaking out for supervision of the financial structure of all corporations engaged in interstate commerce, graduated income and inheritance taxes, workmen's compensation laws, the regulation of woman as well as child labor, and a more extensive conservation program. He was also urging the adoption of the initiative, referendum, and recall, direct primaries, and restraints on the power of the judiciary.

The liberal assault of this first decade of the twentieth century was largely verbal. True, some headway was made in terms of national legislation: the Hepburn, Meat Inspection, Pure Food, and Employer's Liability acts for example. For the most part, however, the Progressives were unable to achieve much in the way of concrete action. The period is significant because liberal progressivism, with its roots back in the agrarian movements of the seventies, eighties, and nineties, was gathering momentum. Progressivism was a more articulate, a more systematic, and a more universal movement than any of its immediate predecessors. While there may be some questions about the genuineness of Theodore Roosevelt's liberalism, and while his contributions in the form of concrete action may not have been quantitatively large, there is no question that he inspired and encouraged liberals, helped popularize their doctrines, and had a tremendous appeal to the middle class throughout the nation. The Progressive movement itself represented a revolt against the control of government by corporate wealth and fear of the consequences of this control for traditional values in the United States. Its concern was for the freedom of the individual in the face of encroachments by big business, for the dignity of the human being in a system characterized by poverty in the midst of plenty, and for the opportunity of the individual to help shape his own destiny.

The Progressive technique was that of recapturing control of political democracy and turning it to the task of regaining a measure of economic and social democracy. It remained for Woodrow Wilson to transform the abstract of the liberal movement into more concrete manifestations. The striking characteristic of Wilson's New Freedom was that it marked the beginning of federal governmental regulation on an appreciable scale. The New Freedom came to embrace a variety of social reforms—lower tariffs in the Underwood Tariff Act, banking and currency reforms in the Federal Reserve Act, the regulation of business practices through the Clayton Anti-Trust and Fair Trade acts. In addition, there was legislation to ameliorate the conditions of farmers, merchant seamen, child laborers, and railroad workers. Specifically, this legislation included the Farm Loan Act of 1916, the La Follette Seamen's Act, the Adamson Act, and the Keating-Owen Child Labor Act. The social legislation of the Wilson period has been characterized as having a dual theme—the steady growth in the value placed upon individual human personality and the shifting of the idea of the public good from the security of the state and established order to the welfare of the mass of the people. As such, Wilson's New Freedom was firmly rooted in the philosophy as well as the method of the Grangers, Greenbackers, Populists, and Progressives who preceded him.

But Wilson also brought something new to the American liberal tradition in this period—the injection of democratic morality into the relations among nations. Wilson attempted to guarantee in the international sphere the same degree of morality and economic freedom that he sought to establish on the domestic scene. The First World War was to give Wilson occasion to express his international idealism. The role the United States assumed during the conflict provided him with the opportunity to give concrete form to this idealism. Desire for peace and pacifism—the maintenance of peace without recourse to war—are good liberal doc-

trines. Underlying each are the humanitarian and rationalist principles of liberalism. For three long years, amidst
pressures on every side, Wilson professed to keep the liberal
faith. While the United States remained, in varying degrees,
neutral, Wilson offered to mediate among the warring
powers, urged a peace conference, and advocated a league
to enforce or protect that peace. When Wilson finally committed the United States to war, it was on the side of "right."
He saw the conflict as one between good and evil, between
morality and immorality, and, in his philosophical justification for the entrance of the United States, saw no incon-
sistency with liberal tenets:

> It is a fearful thing to lead this great peaceful people into
> war, into the most terrible and disastrous of all wars,
> civilization itself seeming to be in the balance. But the
> right is more precious than peace, and we shall fight for
> the things which we have always carried nearest our
> hearts, for democracy, for the right of those who submit
> to authority to have a voice in their own Governments,
> for the rights and liberties of small nations, for a universal
> dominion of right by such a concert of free peoples as
> shall bring peace and safety to all nations and make the
> world itself at last free.[2]

In his Fourteen Points message to Congress, Wilson attempted to spell out more precisely his hopes for the outcome of the war. His Fourteen Points embraced open covenants, self-determination of nations, removal of economic
barriers between nations, and an association of nations to

[2] Albert Shaw (ed.), *The Messages and Papers of Woodrow
Wilson* (New York: George H. Doran Co., 1924), I, 382–83.

guarantee political independence and territorial integrity.

In view of Wilson's achievements on behalf of liberalism, it seems ironical that his administration should have ended on a note of reaction. Such was the case, however, and the atmosphere of the country in 1920 was characteristic of the entire decade which followed. It was a decade of reaction against internationalism, of disillusionment with democracy, and of the materialism of prosperity. Coupled with this reaction was a lack of liberal leadership. The postwar period saw the death of the outstanding leaders of the liberal movement—first, Theodore Roosevelt; then, Woodrow Wilson; followed by Robert M. La Follette; and, lastly, William Jennings Bryan. Their passing seemed to many to emphasize the end of a political epoch. In 1920, Oswald Garrison Villard wrote in the *Nation* that "we have witnessed not the beginning of a new era of liberal domestic reform of which Woodrow Wilson seemed to be the prophet; we have witnessed the end of the old system and have no exact light as to just what shape the new is to take." The spirits of most liberals throughout the twenties were disheartened and were not to be revived until they had first hit a new low, resulting from the stock market crash of 1929 with its accompanying misery and degradation for millions of people. Out of the crash, however, was to come new hope for the liberals and a fresh impetus to the American liberal tradition in the name of the New Deal.

There was little new about the premises upon which the New Deal was based—recognition of the abuses of corporate wealth and the inadequacies of the economic and financial systems; the use of governmental authority to intervene in the interests of mass welfare and the adaptation of governmental machinery to this end; and, eventually, acceptance of the interdependence of nations and American leadership in world affairs—and all had a familiar ring. They were reminiscent of populism, progressivism, and the New Freedom. In embracing domestic measures dealing with such subjects as conservation, social security, increased regulation of transportation and public utilities, aid to agriculture, labor legislation, reform of banking and stock market practices, and an attack against big business and monopoly, the New Deal was echoing voices of the past such as Bryan, La Follette, Theodore Roosevelt, and Woodrow Wilson— champions of the American liberal tradition. Franklin Roosevelt's ultimate objectives and method were similar to theirs, namely, the restoration of traditional American values within the context of the democratic process. Roosevelt sought not the imposition of a new economic and political system but rather a system of private enterprise subject to such regulations imposed by democratic processes as were necessary to provide freedom and opportunity for a majority of the American people.

In the international sphere, Roosevelt followed Wilsonian concepts. While Wilson's hopes and ambitions in this area were far from realized in his time, the internationalism he nurtured was to become a permanent aspect of American liberalism. At least one of his hopes was to become a reality through Roosevelt's efforts. American participation in an international organization devoted to the maintenance of world peace and security is now an accomplished fact; and this same organization has adopted a creed which shows a striking parallel to that of American liberalism from the 1870's on. It reaffirms "faith in fundamental human rights, in the dignity and worth of the human person," and it dedicates itself to the "promotion of the economic and social advancement of all peoples." The method, too, is that of the American liberal—the use of governmental machinery, in this instance international machinery, to achieve the desired ends.

Thus the course of American liberalism in the period from the late 1800's to the late 1930's—roughly a half century—was one of steady development interrupted only by the seeming eclipse of liberalism during the twenties. It is to a consideration of that decade that the remainder of this volume is devoted, for the breath of liberalism had not been completely snuffed out by World War I and the usual postwar reaction. Moreover, in its values and in its methods it displayed a close affinity to the more distinct and popular movements which were its predecessors and immediate successor. As John Chamberlain remarked so adequately in his *Farewell to Reform*, "A broad social movement always has a deep continuity, which, though it may go underground for a time, must inevitably be present for the tapping if the imaginations of men are to be touched." [3]

Liberalism *was* present in the twenties, and all of its champions were not driven underground. A few were most vociferous. Among these was Oswald Garrison Villard, who, as an outspoken liberal in the twenties, seemed out of tune with his times. It was once said of him that he did not belong to that decade at all. Harold Laski has commented that Villard seemed to combine "the remains of the spirit of Theodore Roosevelt's Progressivism with a sympathy for the objectives of Bryan's Populism." [4] Freda Kirchwey,

[3] John Chamberlain, *Farewell To Reform* (New York: Liveright Publishing Corp., 1932), p. 201.

[4] Harold Laski, *The American Democracy* (New York: The Viking Press, Inc., 1948), p. 650.

Villard's successor on the *Nation*, claims that he called for a New Deal program before Roosevelt was even in the capitol in Albany. But the Progressive movement had ended, and the New Deal had not yet begun. Villard, it seemed, was betwixt and between in his political outlook. Herein lies his value to the liberal cause. As has been said of Bryan, Theodore Roosevelt, La Follette, and Woodrow Wilson, so might it also be said of Villard that he was one who touched hands with the past and in his turn helped "to create a situation, in terms of word and deed, calling for new systematic thinkers, new pathologists of the democratic spirit." [5]

[5] Chamberlain, *op. cit.*, pp. 200–201.

CHAPTER III

A Liberal's Concern for Individual Freedoms

THE CORE OF liberalism, historically, has been liberty or freedom. It was in the hope of achieving freedom that political democracies were born. The objective was a form of government best suited to guarantee to the individual maximum freedom from arbitrary and unlimited authority. Self-government seemed to offer the best solution.

Long considered a basic condition of successful self-government has been freedom of thought and expression. Only through the free exchange of information, ideas, and opinions can intelligent and wise decisions be made by those who were intended to be the ultimate source of political power. So long has free speech, press, and assembly been recognized as vital if self-government is to be more than just an empty form that Oswald Garrison Villard, writing in the mid-twenties, was moved to comment; "My subject is such an old one as to make it a ground for wonderment that in this day and generation we should still have to be making pleas for freedom of thought and freedom of the press." Villard reaffirmed their necessity to the maintenance of self-government. "There is only one way to safeguard the Republic to which we all are so devoted," he declared. "Give us a free press, and free vehicles of expression for every possible suggestion or proposal for the advancement of our national life. Shut up the streams of criticism, censor free public expression in the arts and in letters, muzzle the press, and we shall be on the road to autocracy, tyranny, oppression and wholesale corruption in the shortest possible time."

This free flow of ideas to which Villard was devoted necessitates tolerance. It was tolerance which Voltaire was voicing in the statement attributed to him, "I abhor every word you say but I shall defend to the death your right to say it." It was tolerance which John Stuart Mill was voicing in that famous passage, "If all mankind minus one, were of one opinion, and only one person were of the contrary opinion, mankind would be no more justified in silencing that one person, than he, if he had the power, would be justified in silencing mankind." To Oswald Villard it was tolerance that was the mark of the true liberal. "What is liberalism?" he asked rhetorically of Princeton's Cliosophic Society. "How shall it be defined? I have met complete reactionaries who wished to lock up everybody who disagreed with them yet still insisted that they were genuine progressives. . . . Liberalism means above all else tolerance . . . . It means the readiness to pay a price for . . . liberty by freely tolerating license and not only license but bad taste and folly in public utterances as well!"

But liberty, it seems, is never completely won. Each generation must win it anew. The generation that came of age in the years 1918–32 was no exception. It came to maturity in the aftermath of the extreme nationalism and intolerance which accompanied World War I. The wartime espionage and sedition laws of the national government had given rise to a new class of prisoners, namely political, and to the imprisonment of conscientious objectors. State intervention in freedom of expression was manifested through peacetime sedition, criminal syndicalism, and red flag laws; through such inquisitions as that carried on by New York's Lusk Committee; and through such persecutions of radicals as characterized the Sacco and Vanzetti case. The intolerance of the twenties which found all dissenters subversive was not restricted to the state and national governments. Demands for conformity were made on every side. Violations of freedom of conscience were indulged by individuals and by such private organizations as the Daughters of the American Revolution, the Ku Klux Klan, and the American Legion.

One believing as strongly as did Oswald Villard in freedom of thought and expression could only find these abuses profoundly disconcerting. Throughout the period he was to wage battle continuously, courageously, and with single-mindedness of purpose against its manifestations of intolerance and consequent suppression of opinion.

Only a few weeks after the United States entered the First World War, Congress passed, for the first time since 1789, an Espionage Act. The most significant provisions of the act were those found in the paragraph which provided that

Whoever, when the United States is at war, shall willfully make or convey false reports or false statements with intent to interfere with the operation or success of the military or naval forces of the United States or . . . shall

willfully cause or attempt to cause insubordination, disloyalty, mutiny, or refusal of duty, in the military or
naval forces of the United States, or shall willfully obstruct the recruiting or enlistment service of the United
States, . . . shall be punished by a fine of not more than
$10,000 or imprisonment for not more than twenty years,
or both.

The Epsionage Act became law on June 15, 1917 and was
amended eleven months later by what came to be known
as the Sedition Act of May 16, 1918. The Sedition Act added
"attempts to obstruct" to the provision of the Espionage
Act relating to the recruitment or enlistment service and
created additional offenses, such as saying or doing anything
with intent to obstruct the sale of United States bonds;
uttering, printing, writing, or publishing any disloyal, pro-
fane, scurrilous, or abusive language, or language intended
to cause contempt, scorn, contumely, or disrepute as regards
the form of government of the United States, or the Constitution, or the flag, or the uniform of the Army or Navy;
advocating, teaching, defending, or suggesting the doing of
any of these acts.

As is apparent on even a cursory reading, almost anything
said against the war or against the conduct of the war was
punishable under the Espionage and Sedition laws. Under
this legislation, 1,956 cases were commenced and 877 persons were convicted.[1] Most of these persons were Socialists,
leaders of the Industrial Workers of the World, or others
who disapproved of the war on ideological grounds. The
two best-known of those prosecuted under these acts were

[1] Zechariah Chafee, Jr., *Free Speech in the United States*
(Cambridge: Harvard University Press, 1941), p. 52 n.

Eugene Debs, leader of the Socialist Party and its presidential candidate, and Victor Berger, a founder of the Socialist Party in the United States and its first representative in the United States Congress.

Among its administrative provisions, this legislation gave the Postmaster General the power to exclude from the mails anything which, in his judgment, violated the acts. It is quite possible that, because of this provision, freedom of press suffered even more than freedom of speech during the war. Various journals were excluded from the mails. Some, like Socialist Victor Berger's *Milwaukee Leader,* were permanently excluded by having their second-class mailing privilege revoked. In other cases, as in that involving Oswald Villard's *Nation,* only single issues were banned from the mails. On some occasions Postmaster General Albert S. Burleson acted on such dubious grounds as adverse criticism of the British Empire or urging that more money be raised by taxes and less by loans.

Villard relates in his *Fighting Years* that at the very outset Burleson made it known that every Socialist paper in the country was in danger of suppression and that Burleson's solicitor, Lamar, admitted that pro-Germanism, pacifism, and "high-browism" were also to be objects of suppression. According to Villard, Lamar was heard to remark, "You know I am not working in the dark on this censorship thing. I know exactly what I am after. I am after three things and only three things—pro-Germanism, pacifism, and 'high-browism.' I have been watching that paper [*New Republic*] for months; I haven't got anything on them yet, but I shall one of these days." [2]

If these were Lamar's main targets, then it was only natu-

[2] Quoted by Villard, *Fighting Years,* p. 357.

ral that Villard, of German extraction and a pacifist, and his *Nation*, enjoying wide circulation among intellectuals, would be suspect. The September 14, 1918 issue of the *Nation* carried an editorial by Albert Nock criticizing the government's choice of American Federation of Labor President Samuel Gompers to travel throughout Europe and report on labor conditions there. Exercising his power under the Espionage Act, the Postmaster General banned the issue from the mails. Villard was told that criticism of Gompers would not be tolerated. "Mr. Gompers has rendered inestimable services to this government during this war in holding labor in line," Villard reports Solicitor Lamar as having said, "and while this war is on we are not going to allow any newspaper in this country to attack him." [3] On Villard's continued protest, Lamar suggested that he remove the offensive page from the *Nation* and the Post Office would then release it. Villard refused. He went, instead, to President Wilson's secretary, Joseph P. Tumulty, and Secretary of the Interior, Franklin K. Lane. At the next meeting of his Cabinet, Wilson ordered the *Nation* released.

Thus rebuked, Lamar proceeded to issue a public statement in which he reported that an anonymous newspaper had suggested that all other newspapers refrain from reprinting the seditious utterances of the *Nation*. Villard was incensed. He wired Lamar:

> I deeply resent your statement given to the press this morning. At very moment you state Nation is in hands of Postmaster General for adjudication you give out a telegram from an anonymous morning newspaper urging that seditious utterances—like those of Reed, Nearing, and The Nation—be not given space in other newspapers.

[3] *Ibid.*, p. 355.

No seditious or treasonable utterance has ever appeared in The Nation or ever will. I resent the base libel on me personally, but I resent more deeply the infringement on the right to criticize policies of the government—a right which is guaranteed by the constitution. How far this right can be limited by arbitrary action of executive officers is whole issue between us and no other.[4]

The ban on the *Nation* was officially lifted on September 18, and Villard was satisfied that not only was justice being done to the *Nation* but that the right of a free press to criticize government policies was thereby upheld.

Villard was ever insistent that the right of the press to criticize governmental policy of necessity extended to times of crisis because of the enhanced power of the executive:

History is against, and precedent, too, the theory that the press in war times shall either be speechless on foreign affairs, or merely the mouthpiece of the ruling powers. There are no statesmen and no rulers under any form of government, so wise, so just and so far-sighted, as to be beyond the need of the restraining power of enlightened journalistic criticism. Hence any situation that results in a country's press being moulded into one form by official act is fraught with danger, for the official then finds himself without a single restraining influence, since in war time parliaments are invariably dominated by the executives.

So far as Villard was concerned, when the press ceased to be critical of public officials, it failed to perform adequately its function in a democratic society. "It is commonplace,"

[4] *New York Times*, Sept. 18, 1918, p. 24, col. 2.

he told the Illinois Press Association, "that without a free press the Republic cannot survive. A press is not free which is captured by the glamour of public office or yields to the power of authority, any more than it is free if it seeks merely to serve big business or the interest of a single class."

Villard himself was severely criticized on occasion because of his failure to remain loyal to men in public office whom he had previously supported. The most striking example was his sharp and bitter criticism of Woodrow Wilson. Villard had been one of Wilson's three closest advisors in the presidential campaign of 1912. He later found himself in disagreement with Wilson over such matters as United States participation in World War I, the Negro problem, woman suffrage, and amnesty for political prisoners. Villard, moreover, did not hesitate to voice his disappointment publicly. He subsequently felt moved to defend himself publicly. In an article in *Forum*, Villard maintained that the choice of an editor was between remaining loyal to principles or to men, and in his view a free and independent press depended upon the former: "But there was a choice between loyalty to a principle and loyalty— or rather, silence in regard to the act of a friend—which was exactly the same act as we had reprobated a hundred times in professional politicians. To have kept silence would have been disloyalty to the friend; it would also have in honor debarred us from criticising any similar act by anybody else." [5]

It was Villard's further contention that a free and independent press was vital to a two-party system. He insisted that such a system was "dependent for its health and

[5] "Loyalty and the Editor," *Forum*, LXXX (August, 1928), 282.

its progress upon an informed and enlightened electorate, constantly exposed to new and, if need be, unpopular ideas by a free, a fearless, and untrammeled press." Villard enlarged upon this thesis in a *Harvard Crimson* dinner address on March 26, 1932 when he complained that

> the business manager . . . is the last to consider that his is a two-party system, based upon the theory that the electorate shall not only be well informed as to what is going on in the world, but shall have spread before it the conflicting political opinions of the rival parties in order that there may be that constant clash of opposing philosophies which the founders of our nation expected would keep political interest at its height, prevent grave political and governmental abuses, ensure reforms and progress, and preserve the personal and public liberties of Americans.

For these reasons, Villard was concerned about the widespread consolidation which was taking place in the newspaper industry because of enormously increased costs of production. Some cities were left with only two newspapers and under such conditions there was little hope that all points of view would be brought to public attention. Villard could envision an even more critical situation. The *New York Times* reports him as commenting that "it would not be unlikely for Henry Ford, because of great wealth, to buy up every paper in Michigan. Then the people of the whole state would draw all their political, social, and economic information from one source. How dangerous that would be!" [6]

[6] *New York Times*, Feb. 2, 1925, p. 22, col. 2.

Returning to the Espionage and Sedition acts, Villard was extremely anxious with the end of the war to have their victims released from jail. His fondest hope was for a general amnesty. Italy had granted one as early as November 19, 1918; Germany had done so even before the armistice; and the French declared it on October 24, 1919. Sentences under British espionage legislation were so short (none exceeding three years) that all of them expired before 1920.

President Wilson, however, was intransigent on the subject of a general amnesty, and pardons for political prisoners had to await the magnanimity of Presidents Harding and Coolidge. Villard's bitterness with Wilson was expressed in his report of the 1920 Democratic Convention in San Francisco:

Not all the pointing with pride that the platform makers at San Franciso can do will obscure the fact that under the administration of the author of the New Freedom, America imprisoned men with conscientious scruples against killing; that it sullied its noble record by creating a new class of prisoners—political prisoners after the manner of Czar and Kaiser . . . . Alas! Our experience in the war and its aftermath shows once more that you cannot lay violent hands upon the chastity of such goddesses as Justice, and Liberty and Righteousness and Freedom of Soul and then expect them to regain their pristine virginity.

The case of Eugene Victor Debs was a *cause célèbre* in the immediate postwar years. Debs was convicted under the Espionage Act of attempting to cause insubordination in the Army and attempting to obstruct recruiting, although he had not actually provoked any such act. He was arrested for a speech made before a State Socialist Party convention in Canton, Ohio, on June 16, 1918, in which he condemned the war as capitalistic and called upon Socialists to do their duty and destroy capitalism. Debs's speech was not designed for soldiers, nor did he urge his listeners to resist the draft; yet the Supreme Court upheld the conviction and sentence, and Debs, at sixty-four years of age, began to serve a ten-year sentence on April 12, 1919, five months after the armistice.

All requests made of President Wilson to intervene on Debs's behalf failed. Wilson is said to have held greater resentment for Eugene Debs than for any other person who openly opposed his war policies. This may be explained in part by the fact that Debs, in pleading his own case at the trial, quoted freely from Wilson's own *New Freedom.* Villard claimed that it was with "utmost vindictiveness" that Wilson refused to release Debs from prison, even though several members of his own Cabinet so urged. Those who felt that Debs had been unjustly imprisoned were persistent in their attempts throughout 1919, 1920, and 1921 to effect his release. The Socialist Party did not desert him either. In 1920, for the fifth time Debs became the Socialist candidate for the Presidency. Running against Warren G. Harding (Republican), James Cox (Democrat), and Parley P. Christensen (Farmer-Laborite), Debs, from his prison cell in the Atlanta Penitentiary, garnered almost one million votes. In that year Villard's *Nation* refused to choose between the Republican and Democratic candidates and urged its readers to vote for either Debs or Christensen. Villard himself voted for Debs. The choice, as he put it, was between "Debs and dubs."

In April of 1921, the use of Cooper Union was denied to a group wishing to hold a meeting on behalf of amnesty for Debs and other political prisoners. Now Cooper Union had long been a free forum. It was at Cooper Union that Abraham Lincoln on February 27, 1860 gave his so-called "Cooper Union Address" which is credited with being largely instrumental in securing his nomination for the Presidency. It was at Cooper Union that Robert Ingersoll made one of his earliest religious addresses attacking the Bible and where Virginia Woodhull defended the rights of women. It was from the rostrum of Cooper Union that many of the early labor organizers made fiery appeals on behalf of unionization. It was inconceivable to Villard that use of the hall be denied the amnesty group. The refusal had been made on the grounds that those calling the meeting were "disloyal." According to the trustees of Cooper Union, one had written an insolent letter to the President of the United States in the presidential campaign of 1916, and another member of the committee attempted to pledge young men not to volunteer for service in the Army and Navy should the United States go to war. Two others were candidates for office running upon the platform of the Socialist Party which the trustees regarded as distinctly disloyal. Villard wrote immediately to H. Fulton Cutting, one of the trustees:

But are you not falling into a common error of confusing loyalty to the country with loyalty to a given undertaking of the administration that happened to be in power? No one thinks of berating my grandfather, William Lloyd Garrison, or James Russell Lowell, or Wendell Phillips, or Abraham Lincoln because they opposed the Mexican War, which they did most emphatically while the country was at war and our troops were fighting on hostile territory . . . . Our entrance into the world war marked a complete departure of policy for the country in that, for the first time in our existence, it became a crime to differ from the administration in power as to what was wisest and best for the people.

It seems to me that if the same tolerance for the present day had been in existence in 1858–60 Abraham Lincoln would have been denied the use of Cooper Union. He, too, was striking at certain property rights . . . . Peter Cooper's idea, as I remember it, was to establish an open forum. If Cooper Union is to be lost for this purpose I for one shall feel that we must move for the creation of an endowment for a hall here in which every American shall have the right of free speech that is guaranteed to him by the constitution, controlled only by the laws governing the rights of speakers.

Villard did what he could to aid and abet all efforts on behalf of Debs so long as they did not partake of violence. He, himself, took every opportunity to speak to persons in high government positions about Debs. In July of 1921, with a group of editors which included William Allen White, he visited President Harding personally and pleaded for the release of all political prisoners. The President admitted that Debs seemed to him a "kindly and good man" but that he was under pressure from the American Legion and others and that he simply could not consider releasing

Debs until the actual conclusion of a peace treaty with Germany.

Needless to say, many of Debs's friends and followers were not content with Harding's position. Debs had then been in jail for two years, and they were becoming impatient with the lack of results from their efforts to free him. They tended to want to take more overt action on his behalf. Villard persistently warned against the use of violence. He wrote to one of Debs's followers, "I do sincerely hope that all thought of picketing will be promptly dropped. Anything else that is peaceful *The Nation* and I will support most heartily." When challenged about what could be done, all peaceful methods having failed, Villard admitted, "I hardly know what to advise." But he continued to urge peaceful means: "If there could be parades of protest in various cities large enough and esthetic enough to make an impression upon the public mind I should favor that plan. I know no other way but to continue to storm at the portals of the great by letters and petitions and delegations of protest until regular business is interfered with."

True to his promise to release Debs upon the negotiation of an acceptable treaty with Germany, Warren Harding released him on Christmas Day of 1921.

The Espionage and Sedition laws of 1917 and 1918 were applicable only in wartime, and in the postwar years there was agitation in Congress for a peacetime sedition law. In 1919–20 the Congress had before it about seventy such bills, including one recommended by Attorney General A. Mitchell Palmer which went so far as to provide punishment for writings which "tend to indicate" sedition. Palmer, in an attempt to enlist the support of the press, sent to the editors of a leading magazine a circular letter in which he stated that his concern was for a menace abroad throughout the land. "My one desire," he claimed, "is to acquaint people like you with the real menace of evil-thinking which is the foundation of the Red movement." Villard's *Nation* promptly published this letter of Palmer's and stood opposed to any peacetime sedition law which would, in Villard's mind, "make individual liberty and individual rights more than ever the gift of capricious bureaucrats."

Following a visit in 1919 to Germany, where he observed at first hand the bloodshed accompanying civil war in both Munich and Berlin, Villard was more convinced than ever that ideas could not be eradicated by sending men to prison. "The United States Senate," he wrote from abroad, "which, according to press dispatches, believes that our government can best be secured in its present form by the enactment of a new espionage act, would do well to take a trip to Berlin at once. The Senators . . . would also learn things which might lead them to alter their views on . . . the value of prisons as checks to the spread of new ideas, be they for better or for worse."

A vigorous stand by the American Newspaper Publisher's Association, of which Villard was a member, has been credited with having been a major influence in the failure of Congress to pass legislation in the twenties extending the Espionage and Sedition acts. Whatever may have been the cause, nothing comparable to them was enacted until the Alien Registration Act of 1940, which extended the provisions of the Espionage Act of 1917 to utterances in peacetime.

In addition to federal wartime espionage and sedition legislation, similar and often more drastic legislation was enacted by the states. As many as thirty-three states did

what the federal government refrained from doing in the
1920's—making sedition in peacetime punishable. The legislation most common to the states consisted of the criminal
syndicalism and red flag laws. An almost uniform criminal
syndicalism law was passed by seventeen states. That of
California, which was typical, defined criminal syndicalism
as "any doctrine or precept advocating, teaching or aiding
and abetting the commission of crime, sabotage (which
word is hereby defined as meaning willful and malicious
physcial damage or injury to physical property), or unlawful acts of force and violence or unlawful methods of terrorism as a means of accomplishing a change in industrial
ownership or control, or effecting any political change."

It was not uncommon for the state criminal syndicalist
laws to provide that imprisonment from one to fourteen
years could be inflicted upon any person who advocated,
taught, aided, or abetted criminal syndicalism; who willfully
attempted to justify it; who published or circulated any
written or printed matter advocating or advising it; who
organized, assisted in organizing, or knowingly became a
member of any group organized to advocate (without necessarily urging this doctrine himself); or who committed
any act advocated by this doctrine with intent to effect a
change in industrial ownership or any political change.
Such legislation was sufficient to send any member of the
Communist Party or other radical organization to prison.
It was directed mainly, however, against the Industrial
Workers of the World, who were accused of using the war
crisis to bring about the downfall of the capitalistic system.
The Wobblies, as members of the IWW were called, felt,
as did the Socialists, that the war represented a sacrifice of
working-class lives for the benefit of the wealthy capitalists,

and they did not hesitate to say so publicly. As a consequence, more than 1,000 Wobblies were imprisoned in the course of two years.

Prosecutions under criminal syndicalism legislation were especially diligent in the State of California. In the five years following its enactment, until August 15, 1924, 504 persons were arrested and 264 actually tried. To Oswald Villard and other liberals throughout the country, many of these convictions under the California law seemed unjust. Villard wrote to the State Prison Board, in February of 1921, pleading for the release of 12 convicted IWW prisoners:

> As I understand it, not one of them has committed any deed of violence nor is charged with anything of the sort, but is merely convicted of membership in the I.W.W. and the circulating of literature of that organization. I am not at all in sympathy with the I.W.W., any more than I am with the Bolshevist agitators in America. I am not even a Socialist, but I do profoundly feel that when America begins to legislate against thought, it places itself squarely alongside of the Germany of Bismarck in 1878 and the Russia of the Czar.

In general terms, the so-called red flag laws, adopted in thirty-one states by 1921, prohibited the display of the red flag as a symbol of institutions—social, political, or economic—not in conformity with those of the United States. California had both a red flag law and a criminal syndicalism law, as did the state of Washington, which also had a statute against anarchy.

New York State, in addition to a red flag law, established a legislative committee, popularly known as the Lusk Committee, which employed a 1902 law against anarchy (passed after McKinley's assassination) to investigate seditious activities. The Lusk Committee interpreted its powers as virtually unlimited in scope. It functioned as a self-appointed police force, utilizing such devices as John Doe warrants, seizure of property, and surprise raids and arrests.[7]

The Lusk Committee included in its investigations foreign language groups, labor unions, social service agencies, civic reform organizations, pacifist societies, and educational institutions. Such well-known individuals as Jane Addams, Louis P. Lochner, and David Starr Jordan were investigated. Oswald Villard apparently had reason to suspect that he, too, might be under the watchful eye of the committee. Not one to be taken unawares, he addressed a letter to Senator Clayton R. Lusk, the committee chairman: "I hear your detectives are coming to hear me speak next Thursday night at the Pennsylvania Hotel. Unfortunately, I am not going to speak about Russia, and will only give to the audience there the report I made on food conditions in Germany to Mr. Hoover, Mr. Lansing and Mr. Lloyd George. But if your detectives still plan to come, I shall be glad to have them ask for me at the door and I will see that they are given front seats." To Villard, the activities of the Lusk Committee were proof that nothing had been learned from history. The Roman emperors, he once wrote, were as certain as Senator Lusk that "the application of brute force would forever end the particular heresies which they were combating. Christianity was to be stamped out by imprisonment and so are Socialism and Bolshevism."

[7] See Walter Gellhorn (ed.), *The States and Subversion* (Ithaca: Cornell University Press, 1952).

In addition to its red flag law, the state of Connecticut passed a drastic sedition law which punished any person who spoke, wrote, printed, exhibited publicly or distributed disloyal, scurrilous, or abusive matter concerning the form of government of the United States, its military forces, flags, or uniforms. This legislation also covered persons who published or circulated any matter which was intended to bring these items into contempt or which created or fostered opposition to organized government. The California, New York, and Connecticut legislation noted above is significant here for two reasons: first, because Villard took particular note of it; second, because it was characteristic of state legislation throughout the country which was turned against radicals of every hue—International Workers of the World, Socialists, Communists, anarchists—few were to escape the Red scare of the twenties. To Oswald Villard, such legislation clearly represented widespread suppression of thought and expression. He was shocked by what he considered the violation of American tradition:

Americans jailed merely for their opinion? Who in the United States of 1900 would have deemed it possible? At that time it was the historic, well-cherished American doctrine that whatever a man thought, whatever he preached, whatever organization he belonged to, he was free to express his views, free to parade his membership in any alliance or society, free to hold any theories he cared to without any interference by the State or any minor authority whatsoever. Only for an overt *act* could he be held responsible, such as breach of peace or a physical assault upon the Government. This was the fundamental theory upon which the American republic was founded.

Villard went on to point out that to silence the voices of radicalism might well shut off progress. "The radical reform of today," he argued, "is usually the accepted custom of tomorrow," and he referred to the enfranchisement of women as a case in point.

The same atmosphere of fear and hysteria, of nationalism and intolerance, which gave rise to the state syndicalism and espionage laws and New York's Lusk Committee touched the judicial proceedings surrounding the prosecution of a murder in South Braintree, Massachusetts, in 1920. The United States Congress had, on October 16, 1918, passed a bill authorizing the Secretary of Labor to take into custody and deport any alien who advocated or who belonged to any organization which advocated the overthrow of the government by force, the assassination of public officials, anarchy, or the unlawful destruction of property. This act was amended in the spring of 1920 to include all aliens convicted of violation or conspiracy to violate any of the wartime statutes such as the Espionage and Sedition acts or the Trading with the Enemy Act. On the basis of this legislation, Attorney General A. Mitchell Palmer instigated criminal proceedings against thousands of suspected radicals all over the country. Wholesale raids against suspected Reds took place, accompanied in general by unlawful searches and seizures, the destruction of private property, and the detention of individuals for long periods of time without access to counsel. Hundreds of aliens were deported, 249 to Russia alone on one sailing of the U.S.S. "Buford." Again, Villard sounded the warning:

If we try to suppress with rigid hand those who would urge a different form of society; if self-constituted mobs

of uniformed men are to become censors of what the
dissatisfied may or may not say; if we deny the right of
free speech, and free thought to the dissenters; then we
are padlocking the safety valve . . . . To let loose an
idea upon the world is often a terrible thing, but still
more terrible is the effort to combat ideas by force and by
incarceration.

This preoccupation of the Justice Department in round-
ing up radical aliens reinforced a general fear of plots and
intrigue to overthrow the government which had pervaded
the country. Boston, Massachusetts, because of its large
proportion of foreign-born, became a center of Red hysteria. It was in this atmosphere that Nicola Sacco and
Bartolomeo Vanzetti were arrested for the robbery and
murder of the paymaster of a shoe factory in South Braintree. Both men were aliens, anarchists, and draft evaders,
and both had been active in organizing strikes among Italian
laborers in the industrial towns of eastern Massachusetts.
They were also in the files of the federal Department of
Justice as "radicals to be watched." On the basis of evidence
which appeared to a number of legal authorities to be extremely weak if not questionable, Sacco and Vanzetti were
found guilty of the murder and robbery. To many, it
seemed obvious that, given the temper of the times, they
were convicted not on proof that they had committed the
crimes but rather because of their alien and radical back-
grounds. Judge Webster Thayer, who presided at the trial,
had publicly expressed his prejudice against the two men.
He refused all motions for a new trial, even though new
evidence was subsequently produced which pointed to a
professional gang of criminals as the killers. There was also

the suggestion of collusion between the Massachusetts authorities and agents of the Department of Justice to secure the conviction of the two men.

During the seven years that Sacco and Vanzetti spent in prison awaiting the outcome of attempts to get a retrial, controversy over the case raged both in the United States and abroad. Oswald Garrison Villard described in his autobiography an incident which illustrates both his deep concern over the Sacco and Vanzetti case and one segment of public opinion abroad, namely British. Ramsay MacDonald, Britain's first Labor Prime Minister and a close friend of Villard's, visited the United States in the spring of 1927 and was a guest at the Villard home. MacDonald was deeply interested in Sacco and Vanzetti and expressed a willingness to discuss their case with Massachusetts Governor Alvan T. Fuller, in whom the power of clemency and pardon rested. Villard arranged for a meeting with Governor Fuller at the State House and both Villard and Mr. MacDonald were asked to be the dinner guests of Governor and Mrs. Fuller. Villard relates that he accepted "with the one thought of Sacco and Vanzetti in my mind. How to steer the conversation in that direction kept me preoccupied throughout the greater part of the meal . . . . Suddenly Mrs. Fuller turned to me and apropos of nothing said: 'What do you think of the Sacco and Vanzetti case?' If ever I was ready to kneel and kiss the hem of a woman's gown it was then." Villard turned the conversation over to Mr. MacDonald, saying "My opinion is of little value but here is a man whose voice is heard around the world." Ramsay MacDonald then explained that some of the most distinguished of Britain's law profession were of the opinion that Sacco and Vanzetti should be released on the grounds that after six years imprisonment under the death sentence they had expiated their sins if indeed they were guilty. Ironically, Governor Fuller was called to the telephone shortly after MacDonald had begun his remarks, and the full effects of his eloquence were lost. Villard insisted that MacDonald repeat his remarks to the Governor later, but he reports that "the retelling under these circumstances was far less impressive and obviously had much less effect upon the Governor than on Mrs. Fuller. I got the impression at the time that the case was beyond the Governor's grasp." [8]

To American liberals the case had become a challenge to the effectiveness and validity of democratic legal processes in the United States. The primary issue became one of whether judicial procedures in the United States were to be applied impartially as a means of protecting human rights or whether they were to be used, in Villard's words, "to implement the fears of the community, to destroy those who fell out of favor with the ruling interests."

As the date set for the execution of Sacco and Vanzetti, August 23, 1927, drew near, liberal intellectuals made a final effort on their behalf. Villard joined with a group which included Robert Morss Lovett, Jane Addams, John Dewey, and Arthur Garfield Hays to form the Citizen's National Committee for Sacco and Vanzetti. On August 9, Villard wrote to Governor Fuller asking him to commute the sentences of the two men. By this time, public opinion had forced Governor Fuller to review the case. He named an advisory committee consisting of President A. Lawrence Lowell of Harvard University, President Samuel W. Strat-

[8] See Villard, *Fighting Years*, pp. 507–10.

ton of the Massachusetts Institute of Technology, and Judge
Robert Grant. The committee reported to the Governor
that, in its judgment, the men were guilty. Oswald Villard
then wrote on August 12, 1927 to President Lowell, who
had acted as chairman of the committee, to ask why mercy
or commutation had not been recommended and appealed
to him personally to urge the Governor to commute the
sentence or pardon the convicted men. Villard based his
appeal first on the dangers of class antagonism which he felt
the case had accentuated: "In my thirty years' experience in
journalism I cannot easily recall anything else in our American life which has so set apart the working classes and their
friends from those that, for want of a better name, are
described as the capitalistic classes." Secondly, Villard called
President Lowell's attention to public opinion abroad and
warned against the animosity already engendered there
against the United States:

> In Berlin, in Rome, everywhere else, there is unanimity of
> sentiment that men who have been in such jeopardy for
> seven years should not now be executed. Mussolini has
> appealed for them—the despot himself . . . . Is it not
> time once more to pay "a decent respect to the opinions
> of mankind?" . . . There is no other civilized country in
> which men could have lain in jeopardy so long, and it
> is that fact, I repeat, which has so stirred Europe. Can
> we not pay deference to this feeling? Must we add to the
> hatreds we have earned in Europe and in South and
> Central America by the conduct of our foreign affairs?

Villard concluded by appealing to Lowell on the grounds
of justice and humanitarianism:

"Vengeance is mine, saith the Lord." Human beings have never suffered when they tempered justice with a little of the spirit of Jesus. The ruthless determination for vengeance which to the rest of the world seems now to typify Massachusetts, is nothing less than horrifying, especially in view of the torture to which these men have been subjected by their being reprieved at the last moment. It is a horrible cat-and-mouse game—a torture to which no human being should be subjected. . . . it revolts the conscience of every humanitarian to keep men in jeopardy like this.

It was not until one month after the death of Sacco and Vanzetti that President Lowell replied, somewhat casually it might seem, to Villard's pleas: "In looking over my letters, I find the one from you of August 12th, and I am not sure whether I have ever answered it." He went on to reject the idea of mercy or commutation on the grounds that, if innocent, they should rather have been pardoned and, if guilty, they deserved to be executed; and in the opinion of the Governor's committee, they were guilty.

Attempts to prove conclusively the innocence of Sacco and Vanzetti were continued for some time. A lawyer's committee undertook to print a complete transcript of the evidence at the trial and the court record of the various appeals. In Boston, the Sacco-Vanzetti Defense Committee centered its attention on collecting and editing the more important letters and statements of Sacco and Vanzetti. The Sacco and Vanzetti National League, with headquarters in New York City under the main direction of Robert Morss Lovett and meeting as late as March 25, 1930 in the home of Oswald Villard, pledged itself to help obtain publication of

the official record, the advisory committee's report, and the
Sacco and Vanzetti letters; to establish Sacco's and Vanzetti's
innocence; to work for reform of the law—law which made
possible a situation in which all motions for a new trial
could go before the trial judge, who might be prejudiced.
The main purpose of this activity was to complete the record
in order that the law might be guided to more effective
justice. Villard stressed this attitude when questioned as to
what possible purpose continued agitation on behalf of the
two men could serve after their death:

> Those of us who believe in the innocence of Sacco and
> Vanzetti happen to be more than ever convinced of it
> because of new information that has come to us . . . We
> believe that their execution was a monstrous miscarriage
> of justice; that it revealed a weakness in the judicial struc-
> ture of the government of Massachusetts according to
> which the facts in the case were only passed upon by one
> judge whose bias was obvious even to the extent of calling
> the defendants "anarchistic bastards" while in the midst of
> the trial. We believe it to be a patriotic duty to agitate
> this question until that defective system is reformed.

To Oswald Garrison Villard, the kind of treatment which
Sacco and Vanzetti received at the hands of the judicial
system of the state of Massachusetts and of the federal
Department of Justice was far more dangerous to our democratic institutions than the political beliefs for which it
can be said with some justification that they were put to
their death. The case had in it the elements which Villard
was confident would rock the foundations of American

liberal institutions, namely "injustice, corruption, malad-
ministration, intolerance, and lack of progress in our public
officials."

The intolerance and accompanying persecution of the
twenties took many forms and had many participants other
than government officials. There were professional patriots
by the hundreds among private citizens and the many patriotic societies which had sprung up throughout the country. Their patriotism took the form of antagonism to Catholics, Jews, Negroes, and aliens. They opposed immigration
and censored textbooks, periodicals and movies. College professors and speakers were screened for their political views.
Deviations from the acceptable conformity of the moment
was labeled "Bolshevik" or "Red," and the speaker's or
writer's loyalty to the United States became immediately
suspect. Villard and his *Nation* became a natural target of
such groups because of their outspoken and independent
views and penchant for choosing the unpopular side of
issues.

The Daughters of the American Revolution, the American Legion, and the Ku Klux Klan were not the least of
those groups which took to themselves the responsibility
for safeguarding, in their own way, American institutions.
Illustrative of the form which intolerance took was the
black list prepared by the Daughters of the American Revolution. Early in 1928 that organization, together with the
Key Men of America, issued a list of persons considered so
subversive of American principles that they were to be
banned from speaking at meetings of the two organizations
throughout the country. The bulk of persons on the list

were individuals whose views on military and naval preparedness did not agree with those of the DAR, who in
Villard's mind took the position that "the question of
adequate defense of our nation should never be debated
by loyal Americans and least of all by members of the
Daughters of the American Revolution." Among those who
were black-listed, to name just a few, were Jane Addams,
Senator William E. Borah, Attorney Clarence Darrow, Morris Ernst, Arthur Garfield Hays, Freda Kirchwey, Representative Fiorello La Guardia, President William A. Neilsen
of Smith College, Mrs. Franklin Delano Roosevelt, Norman
Thomas, William Allen White, and, of course, Oswald
Garrison Villard.

To Villard and his staff on the *Nation,* the situation had
elements of humor which they proceeded to exploit. The
Nation organized a Black-list Committee, composed of
Clarence Darrow, Morris Ernst, Arthur Garfield Hays, and
Freda Kirchwey, which issued invitations to those people
on the DAR list to attend a "Black-list Party." Invitations
were addressed to "Dear Fellow Conspirators" and read in
part:

> We notice that your name appears on the Roll of Honor
> drawn up by the Daughters of the American Revolution
> and their allies, the Key Men of America. Some call this
> Honor Roll a blacklist. It includes United States Senators,
> Communists, ministers, Socialists, Republicans, editors,
> housewives, lawyers—most of us, in fact. You may bring
> your friend if you can prove that his name appears on
> any blacklist. Otherwise he will not be admitted . . . .
> Members of your family may come; we assume them to
> be at least slightly tinged from association with you.

The letter closed with "Yours to make the world safe for humor," and was signed by the *Nation's* Black-list Committee. Special invitations were sent to such dignitaries as President Calvin Coolidge, New York's Governor Alfred E. Smith, Mayor James Walker, and Mrs. A. Brousseau, national president of the DAR. As many as one thousand persons attended the party held at the Level Club on May 9, 1929. Many others wired and wrote of their disappointment at not being qualified to attend because of the absence of their name on the DAR list. Heywood Broun, for example, was reported in the *New York Times* as being "incensed" that his name was omitted.

Despite efforts to turn the matter of the black list into a farce, its serious overtones could not be dismissed lightly by Villard. To ban speakers merely because one disagreed with their point of view was clearly a suppression of free speech, and to identify those who differed from you as disloyal was invidious:

Be good and you'll be lonesome was an old joke. Be a D.A.R. and be in cold storage; be happily immune from wicked new ideas and from ever hearing one word with which you do not agree . . . . It is certainly entirely un-American not only to deny others the right to speak, but to seek to tarnish their characters merely because of differences of opinion, without giving those attacked a chance to defend themselves and to be heard. It is a most obnoxious kind of censorship because it is secret and irresponsible and gets into the light of day only by accident.

The Daughters of the American Revolution, however, were a relatively mild threat to individual liberties in the

twenties compared with the Ku Klux Klan and the religious
and racial intolerance which it fostered and encouraged in
the name of Americanism. "One has only to think of the
rise of the Ku Klux Klan," Villard reasoned, "with its determined warring upon Negro, Jew, Catholic and foreigner,
or to realize the tremendous development of religious prejudice and hostility in America of late, to appreciate how
dangerous to American liberty are the precedents thus
established."

In upholding "pure Americanism," the Klan resorted
to physical violence—particularly against Negroes—to the
boycotting of Jewish merchants, and to discrimination
against Catholics in housing and jobs. One of the most
disturbing aspects of the Klan problem was the degree of
political power it was able to build in many of the southern
states and several midwestern and far western states. Particular among these were Oregon, Oklahoma, Texas, Arkan-
sas, Indiana, Ohio, and California.[9] The Klan is credited
with having been of considerable influence in defeating
the presidential nomination of Governor Alfred E. Smith of
New York at the Democratic National Convention of 1924.
The convention divided almost evenly between anti-Klan
delegates and delegates who were either pro-Klan or opposed to openly disavowing it. The Platform Committee
refused to condemn the Klan as did the convention itself,
although the amendment to the platform proposed by the
anti-Klan forces was defeated by only one vote. When it
came to nominations, a deadlock ensued between Al Smith,
champion of the anti-Klan forces, and William Gibbs Mc-

[9] See John M. Mecklin, *The Ku Klux Klan* (New York: Harcourt, Brace & Co., 1924).

Adoo, choice of the Klan. On the one hundred and third
ballot, a compromise candidate, John W. Davis, was nominated. Villard's impression of the convention was that it
was more concerned about party unity than rights and
justice. "We were treated once more," Villard wrote of
the convention, "to whining appeals not to disrupt the party,
to remember the innocent but misled members of the Klan
whose motives are so good and so high and patriotic that
they have to express them by skulking around at night in
masks and nightgowns and discriminating against equally
worthwhile or better Americans who happen to be Negroes,
or foreign-born, or Catholics or Jews."

The Republican National Convention of 1924 also refrained from taking a stand against the Klan. According to
Villard, its denunciation of the Klan did not go beyond
"such glittering generalities that the here assembled klans
and kleagles may return to their hometowns with absolute
satisfaction." Both major-party platforms side-stepped the
Klan issue. The Republican platform made no reference
whatever to it; the Democratic platform pledged the party
to the maintenance and defense of the First Amendment
and added only, "We insist at all times upon obedience to
the orderly processes of the law and deplore and condemn
any effort to arouse religious or racial dissension." In Villard's view, the Republican Party best reflected the interests
of the Klan. "If the Klan voters are going to vote in accordance with the attitude of the two conventions," he
explained, "they will vote the Republican ticket because
the decadent Republicans side-stepped the issue without
debate." Ensuing events tended to reinforce his opinion.
In August of 1924, John W. Davis denounced the Klan

publicly by name, as had Robert M. La Follette, the Progressive candidate. Calvin Coolidge was to maintain an unbroken silence on the subject throughout the campaign.

Despite disapproval of the objectives and methods of the Klan, despite the fact that the Klan infringed upon the rights and freedom of others, Villard would not deny it those same rights. Unlike the DAR and the Klan, Villard would not deny those who differed from him their right to express their opinions. Thus he was consistent in his adherence to the principle of toleration:

> The Klan itself has on numerous occasions been deprived of its legal right of assembly. The K.K.K. is surely not much less out of place in American life than the I.W.W. Yet both of them are, according to every American tradition, entitled to every right guaranteed by the Constitution, precisely as our Rotarians, our Chambers of Commerce, or our patriotic societies which, to many Americans, represent the acme of conservatism and reaction.

The patriotism of the war years embraced a compulsive hatred and intolerance of the German people and their government as well as anything which could be associated with Germany in any way. As a consequence, the teaching of German was halted in many public schools; German operas were boycotted; the statue of Frederick the Great was removed from a Washington, D.C., park; and many other manifestations of hatred were indulged.

Villard's German background, coupled with his pacifism and internationalism, made him a ready victim of suspicion and accusations of disloyalty, not only during the war but also in the period of reaction which continued throughout the twenties. Needless to say, many of those who questioned Villard's fidelity were misinformed or misguided, but it is possible also that they were either ignorant of the man's true position on the controversial issues concerning the war or unable to comprehend those convictions which motivated Villard. Persons like Dr. Raymond Alden of Stanford University, who, in 1918, questioned Villard about his rumored "pro-Germanism," were apparently unfamiliar with the publicly stated and publicized views of Villard. As early as 1915, the *New York Times* reported Villard's disapproval of the nationalistic, German-American groups which were springing up throughout the United States. He attacked the development of a political solidarity among German-Americans and warned that "to allow such nationalistic groups to develop here as they did in Austria-Hungary would be most disastrous."[10] Villard made it clear that there could be no divided citizenship, loyalty, or allegiance under the American flag.

By 1917, German groups had taken note of Villard's attitude toward them and had become antagonistic. Named to an honorary committee of one hundred sponsoring a Teutonic Charity Bazaar, Villard was soon dropped on the grounds that he was outspoken in his sympathy for the enemies of the Central Powers. The bazaar, it seemed, was designed to aid the war sufferers of the Central Powers.

In the fall of 1917 the *Chronicle Magazine* undertook to select from *Who's Who* and the *Social Register* the names of persons of German birth or descent, to whom a letter was addressed asking them to affirm their loyalty to America. Villard was among those selected, and the *New York Times* publicized his reply, which unequivocally stated his

[10] *New York Times*, Jan. 30, 1917, p. 5, col. 1.

loyalty to the United States. "While I am proud of my German blood and my German grandfather," he wrote, "and the fact that my relatives were revolutionists against the sort of thing that is now going on in Germany (had they had their way there would have been a republic in Germany in 1848), there has never been one moment in my life when I have been divided in my allegiance to the United States." [11] A few months later, Villard was called upon to defend his position to Stanford's Dr. Alden and wrote, "I want nothing so much as to see the Kaiser and all his crowd chased out. Germany I consider to have been defeated the day she entered Belgium—defeated in the realm of morals, in the public opinion of the world, according to every standard of ethics and morality."

In spite of his public and private pronouncements of loyalty to his country, and in spite of his pleading for and defense of freedom of thought and expression as traditional American liberties, Villard found himself, months after the war was ended, banned from speaking in some parts of the country and mobbed in at least one city where he succeeded in getting the platform. The latter incident occurred in Cincinnati, Ohio, early in 1921 and is an excellent illustration of the intolerant behavior of private individuals and groups in those postwar years.

Villard had accepted an invitation from the Women's City Club of Cincinnati to speak before a joint meeting of the City Club and the Women's City Club. A week in advance of his scheduled address, opposition began to form as petitions of protest, which, according to press reports, contained the names of hundreds of well-known women.

[11] *Ibid.*, Oct. 1, 1917, p. 14, col. 4.

The petitions originated with the Women Voters League of Cincinnati, and they charged Villard with continuing to advocate pacifism after the United States' entry into the war, with opposition to the draft as a measure necessary to bring the war to a successful conclusion and with support of the cause of radical conscientious objectors. Within the space of four or five days, the Literary Club, which rented its rooms to the City Club for weekly meetings, had refused to allow use of its quarters for Villard's speech; the Lions Club unanimously voted its objections to his appearance; the Cincinnati and Covington, Kentucky, chapters of the Daughters of the American Revolution added their voices to the protest. There were resignations from both the City Club and the Women's City Club. When Attorney Robert L. Black resigned from the City Club, he undoubtedly reflected the feeling of many in commenting that "during the war Villard stood for pacifism and against conscription. His name appears on Dr. Fuehr's list of American citizens favorable to Germany. Recently he has publicly defended Roger Baldwin, convicted as a draft evader and next friend to yellowest conscientious objectors." [12] Attorney August A. Rendig, Jr., resigned merely because he found Villard "un-American." [13]

Meanwhile, however, a counteroffensive got under way. A labor union leader commended the City Club for its backing of Villard, and petitions supporting his address were initiated by those who, even while disagreeing with Villard, were concerned for freedom of speech. The City Club and the Women's City Club protested against the "unfairness

[12] *Ibid.*, Feb. 4, 1921, p. 3, col. 2.
[13] *Ibid.*, Feb. 9, 1921, p. 7, col. 1.

and un-Americanism" of various hotels and public halls which had barred Villard from delivering his lecture on their premises. Villard himself wired a defense:

> The charge of disloyalty is absolutely absurd on its face. My book on Germany was the first published by any American after the war began attacking the German position and denouncing invasion of Belgium and declaring Kaiser must go—this in January, 1915. I am proud to recall that Bernstorff, the German ambassador, declared my opposition hurt the German cause more than that of any American journalist. Had I been disloyal I should not have been allowed to go on publishing the *New York Evening Post* and other papers after we got into the war, I would not have been given my passport immediately after the armistice and urged to go to the peace conference.

When Villard made his address that February 11 in the auditorium of the Women's City Club, a crowd of men attempted to storm the doors of the Club but were turned away by an alerted police. Villard was then spirited out of the city by auto to avoid the railroad station which was reported as being surrounded by patrolling Legionnaires.

Villard later blamed Cincinnati's press for stirring up the agitation against him. He had spoken in Cincinnati on the previous January 30 with no opposition whatever, but after that appearance the forces of reaction had set in. He quotes the Cincinnati *Tribune* as saying of him, "He did what he could to make the entrance of the United States into the war a failure abroad and calamity at home. He still preaches his damnable doctrines." The *Tribune* then added a note on the inexpediency of tolerance. There were "momentous occasions" in a nation's life, it posited, "where to tolerate other than one universal opinion, conviction, judgment, is to tolerate treason." [14]

When Villard returned to Cincinnati to speak some ten years later, it was in a friendlier atmosphere. By that time he had traveled in Russia, had written about what he saw there, and had been duly characterized by a Russian reviewer of his writings as "a one hundred per cent American, . . . entirely uninfected with Marxism and . . . chock full of American capitalistic optimism . . . . He went back home to America the same peaceful bourgeois as when he set out on his venturesome Russian trip."[15] Thus damned by the Russians, Villard became much less vulnerable to criticism at home.

Villard's concern over criminal justice throughout the twenties was not confined to the kind of defective judicial system which could send Sacco and Vanzetti to their deaths without a retrial in the face of new evidence, nor to haphazard arrests of aliens and even foreign-born American citizens by the Department of Justice. There were other elements of criminal justice which commanded his attention. He threw his voice and that of the *Nation* into crusades against lynching, the third degree, and capital punishment and in support of prison reform.

Between 1900 and 1920, almost 1,500 persons were lynched in the United States. Considerable agitation for federal legislation to control this abuse of the individual's right to due

[14] Quoted by Villard, *Fighting Years*, p. 476.
[15] See the *New York Times*, Feb. 23, 1930, sec. III, p. 3, col. 3.

process of law resulted. In 1922 the so-called Dyer Anti-Lynching Bill was before the Senate. This proposal would have given federal courts jurisdiction to act where state courts failed to act against persons suspected of participating in lynchings. Villard was strongly in favor of passage of this bill and, particularly in his capacity as vice president of the National Association for the Advancement of Colored People, waged a campaign for its passage. The bill was eventually defeated in the Senate by a filibuster of Southern Democrats, but to Villard the campaign had served at least one purpose—that of focusing "public attention upon the greatest disgrace to America as it had never before been focussed in the South, hitherto all too ready to think that protests against lynchings were merely a symptom of Northern ignorance or ill will."

As for capital punishment, Villard was opposed to it as both a form of punishment and a preventative of further crime. No one, in Villard's view, had the right to deprive another of his life, and capital punishment was ineffective as a crime deterrent. "It is not a deterrent," he argued before a committee of the New York State Legislative Assembly, "it is a survival of barbarism, and . . . it violates the sanctity of human life . . . . Human life is inviolable because it is one thing that once destroyed can never be restored . . . . As for the deterrent effect, what could be more absurd than to maintain it decreases murder . . . violence begets violence, and murder murder." Villard's fight against capital punishment, like his campaign against lynching, however, was not to become one of his successful crusades.

Widespread usage of the third degree, in New York City in particular and throughout the country generally, also moved Villard. To him, the third degree was contrary to a number of principles of traditional American justice. It presupposed a person guilty, rather than innocent until proved guilty; in substance it permitted the examination of a person without counsel present; and it violated the sacred duty of the arresting officer to hold the body of the prisoner inviolate. Villard took the position that public officials on all levels of government and members of the legal profession should take it upon themselves to put an end to the violations of state and local law and the Constitution of the United States which the third degree embraced. "Let the physicians of the law," he argued, "first heal themselves." As time went on without tangible results and he began to spend wakeful nights over the issue, Villard began to look to other solutions. He wrote to the secretary of the New York City Bar Association:

> Frankly, the failure of the Bar Association to move in the matter of the third degree is beginning to get my goat, for the torturing is going on every day. My plan is to go ahead soon in the formation of a group of fifty or a hundred men prominent in New York to address a letter of protest to the Bar Association and the County Bar Association, demanding action and to give this letter to the press. I hate to take this step, but the fact is something *must* be done soon. This whole thing is so much on my mind that it woke me up at four o'clock this morning, and would not let me go to sleep again until just before it was time to get up.

Villard was devoted to the concept that the individual in a free society is entitled to the maximum degree of freedom consistent with peace and order and the public safety. Consistent with this doctrine, he opposed government regulation of morals. "If I were dictator," Villard once somewhat facetiously maintained, "I should remove from the statute books by one stroke of the pen every law regulating the private morals of individual citizens. I should declare that, however men and women behaved in their relations with one another, it was their own affair save where the public peace was disturbed." Taking swimming in the nude as an example, Villard once argued that this was plainly a question of good taste and athletics as well as custom and reiterated that "within the limits of public order the individual should be left absolutely free." Villard decried what he considered the tremendous faith of Americans in the magic of the law as evidenced by the mass of statutes passed throughout the United States in any given year, and he was particularly dubious of those which attempted to regulate morals. "There is no greater fallacy," he exclaimed, "than that of control of morals by law. I am unalterably opposed to censorship of any kind and variety and believe that we must learn that the price of liberty is a certain amount of license."

Specifically, Villard was critical of laws making adultery a crime and of a White Slave Law which was not only ineffective but only resulted in fostering the further offense of blackmail. He pointed to the "hypocrisy" of United States statutes which banned immigrants who may have engaged in extramarital relations. "Just as if," cried Villard, "there were not next door to Ellis Island, on Manhattan, a hundred or more thousand couples living in extra-marital relations."

It should, perhaps, be pointed out here that Villard's opposition to governmental intervention in the area of extra-marital relations was accompanied by a defense of birth control. He advocated the distribution by the government of all the necessary information without charge to the individual. He also favored the eradication of any distinction, legal or social, between children born out of or in wedlock. As for divorce, argued Villard, it ought to be granted simply on mutual consent.

It should also be noted that Villard's criticism of the shortcomings of the White Slave Act did not preclude his favoring the rigid control of the exploitation of the bodies of women for the gain of individuals. Neither did his views on freedom from governmental restraint in the moral sphere include permitting free traffic in drugs. He justified the rigid control of the sale of narcotics because they were a danger to the physical and mental health of the individual and made him ultimately a burden on society, for drug addicts often became public wards.

For much the same reason, Villard advocated not prohibition but control of the dispensing of alcohol "to control the drink habit, so men should not profit by catering to that appetite of their fellow-men which undeniably has done more than any other one thing to fill our jails, our hospitals, and our asylums." Villard's position on prohibition became somewhat nebulous or ambivalent, however. He did not drink, but he was a member of a social class which enjoyed alcohol within limits which Villard found acceptable. When it came to the working classes, however, Villard found himself in agreement with those who considered alcohol an evil. Of his dilemma, Villard once commented privately, "I have never had a problem more difficult for an editor to face."

The administration of the Volstead Act, which went into effect on January 20, 1920 to implement the Eighteenth Amendment, was a failure. The national government did not have enough personnel to control the various sources of alcohol—medicinal liquor, home brew, smuggled liquor, industrial alcohol, illicit stills. In addition, literally hundreds of thousands of people simply refused to accept the law as binding. Villard himself did not take a positive stand on recognizing the law as binding. When queried by a *Nation* reader as to whether or not he would obey the law, Villard replied that, while he *would* obey the Prohibition Law, "I should probably violate any law compelling me to take part in a war, and I undoubtedly would have violated the fugitive slave law as did my grandfather and his anti-slavery associates." What Villard was implying was that obedience to the law is a matter of individual conscience. As a teetotaler himself, he could not claim the right of conscience in disobedience to the Prohibition Law, but he inferred that others might well do so. He made this point of view explicit in 1929, when public opinion against prohibition had become more crystallized: "As to violations of the Prohibition law, my attitude is just this: I think that conscience is above the law and that anyone whose conscience is revolted by a law is entitled to violate it, provided he is willing cheerfully to pay for it." Villard concluded by warning that "those who pretend that their violation of the Prohibition law is due to conscience had better make sure that they are not confusing their consciences with an appetite or habit."

Although Villard recognized that to many persons prohibition was a serious moral issue and that to others it was a matter of personal liberty, he felt compelled to point out with some bitterness that many of the latter were not as vigilant of violations of the more important freedoms of speech, press, and political thought of their day as they were of their freedom to imbibe alcoholic beverages.

CHAPTER IV

Noblesse Oblige:
A Liberal Interpretation

CHARACTERISTIC OF THE liberal movements of Europe in the nineteenth century was a kind of *noblesse oblige*—an effort on the part of members of a privileged class to have their privileges extended to others. Gilbert Murray reminds us that "It was people who had the vote who worked to have the franchise given to the voteless; Christians worked for the emancipation of the Jews, Protestants for the emancipation of Catholics, members of the Church of England who abolished the Test Acts. . . . always a privileged class working for the extension of their privilege, or sometimes for its transformation from a privilege into a common right of humanity." [1]

Oswald Garrison Villard called attention to the fact that there was a notable lack of this characteristic among the privileged order of his day. Writing in the prosperous business society of the twenties, Villard held that the aristocracy of wealth obligated, that wealth should bring with it a sense of responsibility to the state and a readiness to

[1] Gilbert Murray, *Liberality and Civilization* (London: George Allen, Ltd., 1938), p. 31.

serve the country. Villard lamented that there was no *noblesse oblige* in the United States, that here wealth did not connote social responsibility and duty as it might. He urged that there were innumerable opportunities for unofficial, if not official, public service. Villard himself, privileged from birth with wealth, education, travel, and social position, fought the battles of the underprivileged, some of whom were, in effect, unable to help themselves. He championed the causes of the Negro, of women, and of the American Indian. He defended the right of Jews and Catholics to hold public office. He battled on behalf of the foreign-born and on behalf of rights for the American worker.

Villard's concern over those groups to whom enjoyment of the normal privileges or rights of a society was denied because of low economic position or inferior social status reflects the individualist, libertarian, and humanitarian aspects of the liberal philosophy. Devoted to the concept of the inherent worth and dignity of the individual, Villard applied it to all individuals—female as well as male, foreign-born as well as native-born, Catholic, Protestant, Jewish, the poor as well as the rich. All humans regardless of class, creed, or color are entitled to the same opportunities in the liberal ideology for realization of their individual potential. It is not strange, then, that a liberal such as Villard would take up the cause of the underdog, would insist on tolerance and minority rights, and would adopt the humanitarian doctrine that each man has a duty—an obligation to concern himself with the welfare of the rest of the human race.

It is perhaps only natural that the grandson of the Great Liberator should have devoted a great deal of time and energy throughout his life to the problem of the Negro in American society. One thing is certain. In Villard's devotion to the cause of the Negro, he felt duty-bound by his heritage. He spoke disparagingly of the fact that other descendants of the abolitionists had abdicated the cause.

One of Villard's most significant contributions to the Negro cause was his service to the National Association for the Advancement of Colored People. The NAACP was founded in the early weeks of 1909 with the alliance of those Negroes participating in the Niagara Movement for full manhood suffrage for the Negro and a group of white persons led by Mary White Ovington, William English Walling, and Dr. Henry Moskowitz, who, motivated by a race riot in Springfield, Illinois, in 1908, sought justice for the Negro. Villard was invited, in February of 1909, to write the call for the conference of Negroes and whites held on Lincoln's Birthday of that year, out of which the NAACP subsequently emerged. About this request Villard commented, "No greater compliment has ever been paid to me."

The call that came from Villard's pen was impressive. It recited the wrongs that Lincoln would find should his spirit revisit the United States on his centenary. He would find the Negro suffering disfranchisement and discrimination in education, in employment, and in transportation. He would find him denied justice in the courts and lynched by the mob. Silence under such conditions, urged Villard, meant tacit approval. He ended by quoting Abraham Lincoln: " 'A house divided against itself cannot stand'; this government cannot exist half slave and half free any better today than it could in 1861, hence we call upon all the believers in democracy to join in a national conference for the discussion of present evils, the voicing of protests and the renewal of the struggle for civil and political liberty."

Subsequently, Villard served the NAACP in a host of ways. He served in a series of official capacities culminating in his election to the vice-presidency in 1931. For years the association enjoyed free use of space in the *Evening Post* building. In the *Evening Post* and later in the pages of the *Nation*, Villard gave the association, and Negro problems generally, considerable favorable publicity, helping thereby to gain many friends for the Negro cause. Conversely, he withheld unfavorable publicity. He refused, for example, to accept for the pages of the *Evening Post* in 1915 a lengthy advertisement on the motion picture *The Birth of a Nation*, which portrayed Negroes in a disadvantageous light. Villard was also continually alert for sources of financial support not only for the NAACP but for the Urban League and the Civil Liberties Union as well.

In 1912 Villard supported Woodrow Wilson in his campaign for the Presidency. At that time Villard was chairman of the board of directors of the NAACP, and the task of convincing its Negro members that a candidate of southern birth would concern himself with the protection of Negro rights was a formidable one. At one point in the campaign, Villard considered it vital that Wilson should make a public statement assuring the Negroes that they would receive equal treatment before the law and that there would be no discrimination in the matter of political appointments should he, Wilson, be elected. Villard's intention was to publish such a statement in his *Evening Post* and in the *Crisis*, the journal of the NAACP. Villard explained in a letter to Wilson the necessity for the statement:

I feel very strongly that nothing important can be accomplished among the colored people until we have an utterance from you which we can quote. They not unnaturally

mistrust you because they have been told that Princeton
University closed its doors to the colored man (and was
about the only northern institution to do so) during
your presidency. They know that besides yourself, both
Mr. McAdoo and Mr. McCombs are of Southern birth,
and they fear that the policy of injustice and disfranchisement which prevails not only in the Southern states, but
in many of the Northern as well, will receive a great impetus by your presence in the White House.

Although Wilson did not respond to Villard's request for
a statement, he did assure a committee of representative
Negroes that, if elected, he would "seek to be President of
the whole nation and would know no differences of race
or creed or section, but to act in good conscience and in a
Christian spirit through it all." [2]

Shortly after Wilson assumed the Presidency, Villard ap-
proached him, again on behalf of the NAACP, with plans
for a National Race Commission to be appointed by the
President for the purpose of making a study and report of
the status of the Negro, with particular reference to his
economic situation. Wilson had the proposal for the Race
Commission under consideration for three months in all
before he finally wrote to Villard, rejecting the plan because
he found himself "absolutely blocked by the sentiment of
Senators; not alone Senators from the South, by any means,
but Senators from various parts of the country." [3]

While Villard was negotiating unsuccessfully with President Wilson with respect to the Race Commission, he heard

[2] Ray Stannard Baker, *Woodrow Wilson: Life and Letters*
(Garden City: Doubleday & Co., Inc., 1931), III, 387.
[3] *Ibid.*, IV, 222.

rumors of segregation among employees of the Treasury Department under Secretary William G. McAdoo. Villard was deeply concerned because during the campaign he had repeatedly assured the Negroes that Wilson would not condone such a policy. Villard tried repeatedly to see President Wilson on matters pertaining to the Negro but without success. Wilson did, however, in correspondence with Villard, verify the fact that segregation was an accepted policy of his administration and that it was in the interest of the Negroes themselves:

> What distressed me about your letter is to find that you look at it in so different a light. I am sorry that those who interest themselves most in the welfare of the Negroes should misjudge this action on the part of the departments, for they are seriously misjudging it. My own feeling is, by putting certain bureaus and sections of the service in the charge of negroes we are rendering them more safe in their possession of office and less likely to be discriminated against.[4]

Needless to say, Wilson's position was not taken lightly by Negro groups and their white champions. Villard and others—John Haynes Holmes for one—addressed mass meetings on the subject. Villard attributed the adoption of the segregation policy to the "innate prejudice of the Southern portion of the Administration," and claimed that Wilson had thus, at the outset of his career as President, needlessly antagonized one-ninth of the population of the country. Villard regarded Wilson's philosophy as wrong, "his democracy gravely at fault. He has given us beautiful and worthy sentiments in his book called *The New Freedom*,"

[4] *Ibid.*, p. 221.

wrote Villard. "But nowhere do we find any indication that his democracy is not strictly limited by the sex line and the color line." [5] Villard was among those who watched bitterly while Negroes were called upon to serve in the armed forces in order to help make the world safe for democracy in 1917 and 1918. "What hypocrisy! What injustice!" he cried. "They were forced to die for the country which was still for them what Wendell Phillips had called it in Abolition days, 'a magnificent conspiracy against justice!' " [6]

By 1928, Villard was noting that the only political party which took a worthy position on the Negro question was the Communist Party. The platform of Robert M. La Follette—whom Villard had actively supported—in the presidential campaign of 1924 had, strangely enough, made no reference to the problems of minorities, no mention whatsoever of civil rights. The New York State Progressive Party in which Villard was active in 1925 adopted a plank which very generally demanded a true equality of opportunity and freedom of development for all races and creeds. In 1928 both the Democratic and Prohibition parties were silent on the matter of civil rights, and the Republican Party restricted its position on the negro problem to adoption of an antilynching plank. "The only party," declared Villard, "that comes out squarely for giving the Negro every right that would be his under the Constitution if his skin were white is the Communist Party, and that is a fact that the older parties had better take note of."

A month after the radio address in which Villard made this statement, Senator Carter Glass of Virginia took note of it and in so doing referred to Villard as "the rankest

[5] Villard, *Fighting Years,* p. 240.
[6] *Ibid.,* p. 241.

negrophile in America." Villard was not at all disturbed by the charge. On the contrary, he wrote Senator Glass that he regretted he could not accept the designation, for "There are others whose services on behalf of freedom and democracy for the American Negro are so superior to mine that I cannot claim the distinction."

By 1929 Villard noted gains in race relations in the South, but at the same time he observed that the "color line" was tightening in the North. Villard called attention particularly to the economic conditions of the Negro: "Everywhere race prejudice, consciously or unconsciously, is the servant of economic serfdom—sharecropping, exclusion from labor unions, peonage, wage exploitation, political chicanery, and the denial of decent housing, decent living, and decent education." Villard concluded prophetically, "It is a far-flung battle line, and he would be absurdly over-enthusiastic who could feel that the issue has been more than joined."

As Villard fought long and courageously for Negro causes, so he fought for the economic, political, and legal emancipation of women, developing the women's rights issue to the magnitude of a major crusade.

Villard's preoccupation with the rights of women was in the liberal tradition, both European and American. In point of fundamental rights, men and women were created equal and were entitled to the same basic privileges in society. In a nation which based its political institutions on the principle of self-government, women as well as men were entitled to participate in that self-government. To the extent that they were disfranchised, that nation was not fully self-governing.

Oswald Villard's very first public speech, made in Bos-

ton, Massachusetts, was devoted to the cause of woman
suffrage, and he refers to it in his autobiography as his
"maiden" speech. Villard was one of eighty-four men who
marched in the first joint suffrage parade in New York in
1911 amidst jeers and rotten eggs. It was in part through
his efforts that the Men's League for Woman Suffrage was
established, and he served on its board of directors.

Woodrow Wilson's opposition to woman suffrage was
a contributing factor to Villard's eventual coolness toward
Wilson and his dissatisfaction with Wilson's liberalism. Wilson was not converted to woman suffrage until 1918. Two
factors have been attributed to changing his mind. First,
two of Wilson's daughters joined the suffrage cause; and
second, he was impressed with the work women had done
during the war. Villard never accepted this explanation.
He was of the firm conviction that Wilson's conversion
was due to political expediency alone, a motive which Villard abhorred. He was sure that Wilson feared that Theodore
Roosevelt would be a nominee for the 1920 presidential
election and would garner the votes of the suffrage states.
As Villard described Wilson, he "liked, as any proper man
should, pretty women and their company but he never had
respect for their intellectual accomplishments or believed
them else than quite inferior to men. Women no more than
blacks figured in his vision of a really democratic society." [7]

Villard's concern for the improvement of the status of
women did not end with the acquisition of the suffrage.
He fought for legal as well as political rights for women.
He fought for civic and professional status for them as
well. Villard was critical of Wilson, for example, because
he had not included a woman in the Peace Conference at
Versailles. He was later to criticize President Herbert Hoo-

[7] *Ibid.*, p. 291.

ver for not appointing a woman to his Cabinet. Writing
to the Right Honorable Margaret G. Bondfield, first woman
Cabinet member and privy councilor in Great Britain, Villard commented, "It will amuse you to know that Herbert
Hoover now says he intended to appoint a woman in his
cabinet but he could not find anyone to measure up to the
office. This in the land of Jane Addams, Frances Perkins,
Julia Lathrop, and all the rest!" With what satisfaction
Villard must have viewed the appointment of Frances Perkins as Secretary of Labor in Franklin D. Roosevelt's first
administration. As early as 1920, Villard was critical of
the major political parties for not allowing women full
participation in their councils. He wrote of the Democratic
National Convention of that year, for example, that only
one woman was allowed to speak and this as "a sop to the
millions of newly enfranchised Democratic voters." In 1931
Villard urged that women be represented at the Geneva
Disarmament Conference to be held in the opening weeks
of 1933. He wrote to Secretary of State Henry L. Stimson,
inquiringly and again prophetically, "Why should not a
woman be represented in this matter? I am sure the women
have the greatest stake and represent one-half or more of
the human race . . . . Some day the participation of women
in international councils like this will, I am sure, be taken
for granted."

During the twenties, the women of America followed up
their successful campaign for the suffrage with demands
for freedom of movement in a number of other areas. They
began to examine critically, for example, the institutions
of marriage, divorce, childbearing, and birth control. Writing in Villard's *Nation* in 1924, Beatrice Hinkle attempted
to explain the moving force behind woman's latest search
for freedom of action and expression: "Women are demand-

ing a reality in their relations with men that heretofore
has been lacking, and they refuse longer to cater to the
traditional notions of them created by men, in which their
true feelings and personalities were disregarded and denied." [8]
Women were attempting to find themselves, to attain a sense
of individuality and fulfillment independent of the opposite
sex.

Villard applauded, encouraged, and abetted all of these
efforts and he was to classify the emancipation of women
as among his more successful causes. He looked upon gains
made on behalf of women not only in his own country but
abroad with satisfaction in 1939, when he wrote:

> We have beheld the complete change in the status of
> women; a Hitler has tried in vain to restrict them to
> *Kinder* and *Kuche*, though not to the church. Women
> can and do conquer as much of the industrial world as
> they desire and they have penetrated deeply into the pro-
> fessions in all enlightened countries. They have captured
> advanced positions in their assaults upon the archaic laws
> which have held them in bondage—with some redoubts
> still to be taken. Woman now knows that her body *is*,
> or should be, her own; that she has rights as to her children
> and, in some countries at least, owns her own property
> free from the control of her husband.

The twenties was a period in which increasing attention
was focused on the problems of the American Indian, and
considerable legislative action was taken on his behalf.

[8] "Women and the New Morality," *Nation*, CXIX (November 19, 1924), 543.

Groups devoted to the welfare of the Indians consolidated themselves in the early twenties into the American Association on Indian Affairs and began to draw public attention to their cause. The Indian Bureau of the Department of the Interior came under such sharp attack on its administration of Indian affairs that in the early twenties it appointed an Advisory Council on Indian Affairs and a Committee of One Hundred Citizens to consider problems of the Indian. Oswald Garrison Villard was invited to become a member of both groups.

The Committee of One Hundred Citizens met in conference in December of 1923. One of the issues before it had been raised in the annual report of the U.S. Commissioner of Indian Affairs of June 30, 1923, and had become the center of public controversy. It dealt with the religious ceremonies of the Indians. The Commissioner reported that he had circulated a letter among the tribes suggesting that less time be given to religious ceremonial dances. The suggestion was seemingly motivated by economic reasons. The ceremonies took the Indians away from their work, sometimes for days at a time, and their fields were thus neglected. And, too, some of the ceremonies required offerings, and individual Indians were known to sacrifice all of their livestock and farm implements. There were those, however, who considered some of the ceremonies immoral; there were others who felt that they imposed hardships on women and children. Others, however, like John Collier, who was later to become United States Commissioner on Indian Affairs, interpreted the issue as one of religious liberty versus "cultural toleration."

At the Conference of the Committee of One Hundred Citizens, William Jennings Bryan put forth a proposal which

in effect embraced governmental suppression of the Indians'
religious ceremonies. Villard was extremely critical and in
his objections adopted basically the attitude of Collier. Villard viewed the proposal as an attempt at conformity, and,
as might be expected, he was unequivocally opposed to conformity. He wrote:

> The curse of "Americanization" is coming to rest upon
> the Indian as upon our immigrants. They must be made
> just like the rest of us in their fear of the future, and they
> must be stripped of all their tribal customs, culture, beliefs
> and arts. If they are not in the course of time made ab-
> solutely to conform to the standards of Main Street in
> Lincoln or Tampa it will not be Mr. Bryan's fault or that
> of most of the missionaries. Fortunately there were brave
> and outspoken words against this proposed outrage.

It was following this meeting that Villard noted, with
regard to what he considered the Indians' fundamental
right to the ballot, that "the same old arguments advanced
against the enfranchisement of negroes and women, were
heard once more." He went on to cite the familiarity of
the argument put forth by one member of the committee
that some of the Indians who were too ignorant to use the
ballot and did not really want it should not have it forced
upon them. Villard noted, too, that the conference took no
notice of denials to the Indians of equal protection of the
laws. Four years later, in his plea for *noblesse oblige,* he
observed that little change had taken place in the status
of the Indians. "The Indians continue," he complained, "to
be robbed, maltreated, denied the rights of citizens such as
a fair trial in court, or the right to will away their property,

or to say where and how their children shall be educated." Here was a great unfinished task for those who would respond to the need for public service.

One of the most discussed public policies of the twenties was that of immigration. The period following the First World War marked the end of an epoch in United States immigration policy. For a century the government had pursued the policy of an open door for immigrants, a policy which the enactment of the quota laws sharply reversed.

In 1897 Congress had passed a bill which, for the first time, embodied a literacy test in the selection of immigrants. President Grover Cleveland vetoed it. Congress renewed its efforts to impose such a test in the Smith-Burnett Immigration Bill of William Howard Taft's administration, but again a Presidential veto stifled the move. In 1915 the Burnett Immigration Bill was before President Woodrow Wilson for his signature. This bill embodied the literacy test and the exclusion of those immigrants who "advocated and taught unlawful destruction of property." Oswald Garrison Villard was among a delegation which appeared before the President to protest the bill. Although the main complaint of the group was the literacy requirement, Villard also expressed opposition to the exclusion of those advocating and teaching the unlawful destruction of property. His opposition was based on the ground that this clause would exclude those seeking political asylum in this country from oppression in their homelands. "As long as forcible revolution is regarded as legitimate the world over," the *New York Times* reports him as saying, "it would be monstrous to say that we should deny asylum to foreigners who might

sit together and dream dreams on our territory of tyrants'
yokes broken at home and foreign despots driven from their
shores. Shall we set a premium on spies and informers?" [9]

President Wilson vetoed the Burnett Bill and another
similar to it in 1915. In 1917, however, a bill embracing the
literacy test was passed over the President's veto. Subsequent amendments provided for the exclusion of "anarchists
and all who favored the over-throw of law and government
by force and violence." It seemed obvious to many that the
literacy provision was a means not of selection but of exclusion of immigrants. The objective seemed to be that of
curtailing the admission of immigrants from southern and
eastern Europe. This became explicit in the Emergency
Quota Act of 1921 and the Quota Act of 1924, which
limited the number of persons who might enter the United
States in any one year from each country and established
quotas which favored immigration from the British Isles
and western Europe.

Villard was bitter in commenting on the seeming lack of
gratitude of a country which "having developed much of
its resources by the brawn of foreigners and become rich
thereby, it was suddenly so purse-proud as to be willing
to cast off the 'Dutchies,' 'dagoes,' 'wops,' Chinese, Irish and
others whom it was once so glad to welcome to its shores."
As for banning those who advocated revolution, Villard
wrote:

> We abolished by law the right of political asylum in
> America and made it a criminal offense to do what the
> Irish are doing today—to plot here for a revolution within
> another country—this in a land which gave such a royal
> reception to Kossuth and raised money by public sub-

scription for revolutions in Greece, Hungary, Italy and heaven knows how many other lands. Nothing could more clearly indicate the change in America—the sudden alteration of our national attitudes towards those struggling for liberty abroad.

Villard was correct in interpreting the new restrictions on immigration as a reflection of a marked change in attitude on the part of Americans toward foreigners. Nationalism accentuated by the war, increasing competition between alien and native laborers, the apparent inability of some immigrant groups to be assimilated rapidly—all tended to contribute to a public opinion favoring further restriction of immigration. To these factors were added some rather specious arguments on the advisability of restrictions. One among them was fear for the safety of American institutions. Thus President Coolidge could argue in his State of the Union Address of 1923 that "American institutions rest solely on good citizenship. They were created by people who had a background of self-government. New arrivals should be limited to our capacity to absorb them into the ranks of good citizenship. America must be kept American." Thus Representative Albert Johnson, chairman of the House Committee on Immigration and Naturalization, could say in 1927 that

Our capacity to maintain our cherished institutions stands diluted by a stream of alien blood, with all its inherited misconceptions respecting the relationships of the governing power to the governed . . . . The United States is our land. If it was not the land of our fathers, at least it may be, and it should be, the land of our children. We intend to maintain it so. The day of unalloyed welcome to all peoples, the day of indiscriminate acceptance of all races, has definitely ended.[10]

Villard, reflecting on the situation, retorted that "If men like Congressmen Johnson, who are now so bent on excluding all aliens from America in pursuit of the narrow, selfish, nationalistic dogma of 'America for those who are already here,' could ever be brought to measure the contributions of some of the thousands who came penniless to these shores in foul-smelling steerage quarters, they would surely be shamed into something different."

Another concern of those who advocated immigration restriction in the twenties was that immigrant blood might dilute the physical, mental, and moral qualities of Americans. This sentiment was implicitly reflected by President Hoover in his first annual message to Congress on December 3, 1929, when he stated that he "hoped that we could find some practical method to secure what I believe should be our real national objective; that is, fitness of the immigrant as to physique, character, training, and our need of service." Then there were those who, like Professor Henry Pratt Fairchild of New York University, tended to ignore the contribution of immigrants in the molding of America and who argued that unrestricted immigration was destroying American nationality, which in essence was the very "soul" of America. "What was being melted in the great Melting Pot," wrote Professor Fairchild, "losing all form and symmetry, all beauty and character, all nobility and usefulness, was the American nationality itself." [11]

[10] Introduction to Roy L. Garis, *Immigration Restriction* (New York: The Macmillan Co., 1927), pp. vii–viii.

[11] Henry Pratt Fairchild, *The Melting Pot Mistake* (Boston: Little, Brown & Co., 1926), p. 260.

Such preachments were a natural consequence of racist ideas which were prominent during the 1920's. Numerous writers of that era developed a theory of the superiority of American Nordicism. They received their rationale and much of their inspiration from Madison Grant, whose volume entitled *The Passing of the Great Race* was first published in 1916. Grant attempted to trace the history of Europe in terms of hereditary impulses, predispositions, and tendencies distinctive of the several races. It was a simple matter for Henry Fairfield Osborn and Charles Stewart Davison to apply Grant's thesis to the United States. Grant himself, observing what he considered an "alarming replacement of the native American," was ultimately led to plead for a halt in immigration: "We have lost our national homogeneity of race, tradition and religion. All we have left of our splendid inheritance is our language. The decline of the native American rural population continues. The birth rate of the native American family is falling, in contrast to the high birth rate of the newly-arrived immigrant." [12]

Oswald Garrison Villard's reaction to such preachments was to point out that "today we are in the position of a man who has risen to a point of vantage by a high ladder, and then proceeds to kick the ladder out from under him so that others may not ascend and take their place beside him." Villard was impatient also with American labor for its fear of competition from the immigrant, and he was contemptuous of what he considered the past exploitation of foreign labor in the United States: "We have admitted foreign labor freely as long as we could exploit it, utilize

[12] In Madison Grant and Charles Stewart Davison (eds.), *The Alien in Our Midst* (New York: Galton Publishing Co., 1930), pp. 22–23.

it to destroy the vastness and conquer great obstacles of nature, open up new roads to empire, and then we have barricaded the doors. The modern Americanism wants a Chinese wall around the United States." Answering those who argued further that certain categories of the foreign-born should be excluded from the United States as "unde-sirables," Villard retorted that the greatest mischief-makers and crooks it had been his duty to "scourge" in his years of service to the public were those with American names. He pointed to Boss Matthew Quay, to Albert B. Fall and Harry M. Daugherty of the Teapot Dome oil-leasing scan-dal, to Colonel Charles R. Forbes of the Veterans' Admin-istration graft scandal, and to Senators William S. Vare and Frank L. Smith who were denied their seats in Congress because of excessive election expenditures. In the face of all these bad examples of Americans, postulated Villard, "we put up bars of ingratitude to our great foreign born and keep heaven knows how many geniuses out."

The restriction and exclusion principles were not the only moves made against the alien in the twenties. In 1926, Secre-tary of Labor James J. Davis recommended the compulsory registration of aliens. An unsuccessful attempt was made to carry out the recommendation with the introduction of two bills into the House of Representatives by James B. Aswell of Louisiana. Those who supported the bills argued that they would prevent "bootlegged" immigration from Canada and Mexico and would give aliens who were in the country legally proof of their legal entry. Those opposed, such as Villard, considered the proposal a violation of per-sonal privacy and a type of police control. "I consider this one of the most vicious bills which I have known for many years," Villard wrote Senators Burton K. Wheeler, Robert

La Follette, Gerald P. Nye, William E. Borah, George Norris, and others of a similar bill in 1930 known as the Alien Registration Bill. "It means the fingerprinting of all aliens and will give the police and reactionary employers complete control over these people. It is the first step in introducing old-time Russian and Prussian police methods into America."

Writing on the one hundredth anniversary of the birth of a great German-American, Carl Schurz, Villard reflected upon the injustice and ingratitude of those who advocated the alien registration proposal:

> As these lines are written the exclusionists in Congress are doing their best to make the immigrant still more an outcast, an object of suspicion and distrust from the hour of arrival, to be deported for offenses which in native-born citizens seem to the public all but harmless . . . . Were Carl Schurz here to celebrate his hundredth birthday that would surely be his plea—justice for and trust in those who, as he did himself, come now to give to the United States a new and a fresh devotion, a quickening of the thinning blood of those who, born into American life and riches, give no heed to the glory or the sacredness of traditions handed down to them.

The various manifestations of intolerance which accompanied the end of the First World War included a hatred of Jews and of Roman Catholics. In the minds of many Americans, Jews were associated with radical economic ideas and the Catholics were about to deliver the country into the hands of the Pope.

Oswald Garrison Villard, consistently the critic of intolerance wherever he found it, not surprisingly aligned himself on the side of Jews and Catholics whenever necessity to do so occurred. Villard was so warm a supporter of the Jew, that he criticized Jews, individually and as a group, for not fighting their own cause more forcefully. Speaking of Adolph Ochs and his *New York Times*, for example, Villard noted, "For not even the Jews, Mr. Ochs' race, has it pleaded as ardently as have others, apparently for fear lest it be further decried and criticized as a Jew paper." The taint of prejudice touched Villard's alma mater, Harvard College, in 1922. Harvard gave consideration to restricting the number of Jewish students to be admitted. Villard was quick to join the opposition to such a move among the alumni but was disappointed with the willingness on the part of Jews themselves to compromise the issue. He expressed his views in a letter to James Loeb: "You will have noticed the fight we are making against its policy but, as usual, we gentiles who are fighting for Jewish rights are handicapped by the fact that so many Jews are willing to accept a compromise—they say it is better to surrender now than to have anti-Semitism in full blast later, and total exclusion from certain colleges. That kind of compromise my Garrisonian training does not let me relish."

One of Villard's primary concerns for Catholics and Jews, as it was for women and Negroes, was that they be allowed to hold public office. To him, discrimination in this area was not only intolerant and undemocratic but un-American and immoral as well. The 1928 presidential campaign in which Governor Alfred E. Smith of New York, a Roman Catholic, was the Democratic candidate provided occasion for great public voicing of anti-Catholicism. Vil-

lard was disheartened by the intolerance of the campaign.
"As for the election," he wrote William Allen White, "I
think it is a very sad one, if only because it offers proof to
the entire world that we are a fanatical and bigoted people."
Villard voted for Alfred E. Smith in 1928 and did so, he
related, solely on the ground that a Roman Catholic ought
not to be denied the right to hold the highest public office
in the United States simply because of his religion. In 1932
he felt the same about the nomination of a Jew, Herbert
Lehman, for the governorship of the state of New York
on the Democratic ticket:

> I am gratified that the Democratic Party dared to nomi-
> nate a Jew for Governor, and it was a great satisfaction
> to see the Protestant Franklin Roosevelt and the Catholic
> Al Smith backing him unqualifiedly for the nomination.
> We have an enormous Jewish population in New York.
> It would be about the most un-American procedure possi-
> ble if it should come to pass that a man could not be
> nominated for the highest office in the State of New York
> because of his race. And this applies to colored men just
> as it does to Jews. The one question is, after all, whether
> a candidate is fit, whether he is honest, whether he is
> trustworthy, whether he is a true democrat, and whether
> he has vision.

Villard's championship of the Jews did not go unnoticed
by them. In suggesting Mr. Villard as recipient of the
Gottheil Medal, awarded annually for meritorious service
to the Jewish cause, Jacob Billikopf asked the editor of the
Detroit Jewish Chronicle, "Do you know anyone in this
country who has fought more valiantly in behalf not

only of the Jews but of racial and religious minority groups?" [13]

Of his admiration for the Jews and his gratitude for the support they gave him over the years in his fight for causes other than their own, Villard wrote that "in this hour of diabolical, un-Christian, psychopathic, anti-Semitic barbarism, I must state the simple truth that if I had not had the support and encouragement of many Jews I could not have carried on in the measure that I did. Their idealism, their liberalism, their patriotism, their devotion to the cause of reform in the time-honored American way, heartened me in the hardest hours." [14]

Relations between labor and management during the World War I years were marked by relative calm. In the interest of national security, labor had refrained from striking and at the same time had been granted wage increases. The postwar years, however, were characterized by a decidedly less compromising attitude on the part of both labor and management. A long series of strikes and lockouts began in January of 1919, some of them accompanied by violence. Among the more important were the strike in the steel industry, under the leadership of William Z. Foster, the Boston police strike, and the United Mineworkers' strike, led by John L. Lewis.

Labor suffered a serious defeat in the steel strike. When

[13] Letter from Jacob Billikopf, June 24, 1938, to Philip Slomovitz, editor of the *Detroit Jewish News*, files of the newspaper. See also editorial praising Villard in the *Detroit Jewish Chronicle*, June 17, 1938.

[14] Villard, *Fighting Years*, p. 529.

public opinion turned against it, a back-to-work movement got under way, and the strike was conceded a failure. At one time during the strike federal troops were used to establish martial law and restrict picketing in Gary, Indiana. The Boston police strike, too, was a loss to labor. Calvin Coolidge, then Governor of Massachusetts, called out the State Guard and requested the use of federal troops. In the face of such odds, the strike was brought to a close. In the case of the mineworkers, the federal government requested and received an injunction which spelled immediate defeat for the miners. Of the government's action in the coal strike, Villard wrote to Emily Balch that "politically the situation is perfectly disgusting and tends to make every liberal more and more of a revolutionist as time goes on. The action of the Government in the coal strike has been simply indefensible. It could not have more deliberately taken the side of the employers. Where shall we wind up when it is all over, Heaven only knows!"

Organized labor suffered other setbacks. The public began to identify labor unrest and leadership with foreign radicalism. As a result, a number of labor leaders were harassed and prosecuted on one charge or another. Management waged a campaign against what it considered the excessive power of unions. Trade union membership, which had increased 96 per cent between 1915 and 1920, began a sharp decline. The depression of 1921, with its accompanying surplus of labor, gave management the opportunity to show preference to nonunion workers. To observers sympathetic to labor, it appeared as though an attempt were being made to eradicate unionism in the United States. In January of 1921, Villard saw reason to comment that "reaction is in full force. The capitalists are taking advantage of the great depression to 'stand labor up against the wall and take everything out of its pockets,' to quote a friend of mine. There is a most determined nation-wide effort to smash the union movement."

From 1919 to 1923, the state of Kansas attempted compulsory arbitration. It forbade strikes in industries which affected the public interest and established a Court of Industrial Relations to decide all disputes which threatened the public welfare. When workers resisted, their leaders were subject to jail sentences. Organized labor bitterly opposed such compulsory arbitration on the ground that labor contracts imposed by authority and enforced by penalties amounted to slavery. Villard tended to agree:

> As a practical proposition the scheme is simply unworkable, and the very existence of a court nominally empowered to determine the conditions under which wage workers must invest their lives acts as an irritant to those who long for freedom. It is time for practical men to face reality; the workers cannot be treated as chattels. Neither can they long be fooled by panaceas which give them a mere illusion of freedom and justice. The basis for industrial peace is an honest recognition of the right of organized workers to an increasing measure of control over industry.

In 1922 railroad shopmen went on strike at the announcement that they were to suffer a wage decrease. Asserting that the strike interfered with interstate commerce and the mails, Attorney General Harry M. Daugherty succeeded in obtaining a restraining order which forbade just about every conceivable activity connected with the conduct of a strike. Villard called the injunction vicious and editorialized about "Government by Daugherty."

That injunction, sweeping as it was, tends in retrospect to dramatize the whole issue of the use of the temporary injunction as a weapon against labor which became so common during the 1920's. Conservative courts, eager to protect private property, issued injunctions restraining labor from such activities as engaging in strikes, assembling to act or organize for a strike, paying strike benefits, engaging in boycotts, picketing, adopting rules against the handling of goods by nonunion labor, and making trade agreements with employers stipulating the employment of union labor only and the production of goods under union conditions. The list is not exhaustive. Temporary injunctions required neither hearing nor trial, but violations were punished as contempt of court. Most strikes were broken before hearings could be held on the question of making the injunctions permanent. Villard pointed out quite correctly that under these conditions labor was helpless. It was futile to think that organized labor could exist if its right to organize and strike could be so restricted. "The very life of unions," wrote Villard, "depends on such activities, and if the state can forbid them the workers are back in the helpless position of the early days of the industrial revolution." Villard proceeded to lecture labor on the duty of civil disobedience:

> What men once endured to abolish chattel slavery some men in the ranks of labor must do to end industrial peonage. The pioneers of labor's emancipation may have to practice the high duty of civil disobedience though they

share the fate of Gene Debs and with him have to test in their own person the truth of Thoreau's great words: "Under a government which imprisons any unjustly the true place for a just man is also a prison. . . . how much more eloquently and effectively he can combat injustice who has experienced a little in his own person."

In 1926 and 1927, the woolen mills of Passaic and Paterson, New Jersey, were the center of extended labor unrest and a fourteen-month strike over low wages and poor working conditions. During those months there were physical clashes between police and strikers. Strike leaders and sympathizers were arrested, and there were indications of abridgement of civil liberties on the part of local authorities. Among those arrested were Villard's good friend Norman Thomas and Robert Dunn, an associate of Villard's in American Civil Liberties Union work. Villard was quick to offer $20,000 bail on their behalf. The Riot Act under which many of the arrests were made was applied to deny freedom of speech and of assembly. Villard, in warm support of the strikers, wired James P. Cannon, secretary of the International Labor Defense Committee, as follows:

In nearly thirty years of active journalism I do not recall a dose of labor trouble in which there has been a worse abuse of authority than this one in Passaic and Patterson. The complete denial of civil liberty ought to make any American who values his birthright rise in protest. The authorities have not only misused their powers in the most arrogant and unconstitutional way, but they have by their partisanship and one-sidedness done everything to incite the strikers, and their refraining from violence in face of brutal police clubbings reflects the greatest credit upon them and their leaders. They deserve all possible moral and financial support.

While Villard was generally sympathetic to labor, he never assumed the attitude of labor, right or wrong. Any method used by labor which hinted at violence, for example, he could not condone. Many of labor's policies he thought were in the best interests of neither labor nor the country. Particular among these were labor's position on immigration restriction and on tariffs. Expressing his displeasure with labor on these issues, Villard wrote a British friend:

> You are quite right about the stupidity of labor as to the tariff, but your crowd are intelligence itself compared with ours. The American Federation of Labor in its annual session has just come out for much higher tariffs, especially on agricultural products. If they had their way, we should immediately enact your Corn Laws. In every respect they are among our greatest reactionaries. They are, for instance, behind the restriction of immigration and the limitation of jobs. I sometimes wonder if there is a single economic fallacy which they have not embraced.

Villard was sympathetic to a strong and independent organization of workers primarily because he considered such an organization a necessary counterbalance to the power of big business in its relation to its workers. He felt a keen sense of injustice at the great divergence of wealth and income which existed in the United States. Villard also looked upon unionism as an additional restraint on a government which might, in the absence of such a force, be either inconsiderate of or unresponsive to the mass of the people. Effective democracy necessitated that the masses have media, apart from the vote alone, by which to guide governmental action, by which to express their needs and desires. He looked upon labor unions as serving as one such medium.

CHAPTER V

Toward More
Political Democracy

"THERE IS NOTHING sacred or sacrosanct about our existing form of government," wrote Oswald Garrison Villard. "It must be modified from time to time as conditions change." Thus Villard reflects a basic characteristic of American liberalism—that of pragmatism, which requires that all social institutions be evaluated in terms of their practical consequences for democratic ideals. In this context, liberals are, as Gilbert Murray has described them, skeptics. "Always," he states, "you will find the great mass of the people believing, the popularity hunters pretending to believe, and the liberals questioning, those accepted traditions." [1] If found lacking, it follows for the liberal that social institutions must be changed. And the American liberal has shown a persistent and confident belief that change, and therefore progress, was always within the realm of possibility. Because he believed in the mutability of institutions, the American liberal has often been described as being experimentally minded in politics, eager to try new approaches which in turn are subject to review and discard. The liberal has little patience

[1] Murray, *op. cit.*, p. 22.

with those who show doubt about the untried. "The mere fact that it has not been done before," Villard maintained, "is surely not a ground for saying it cannot be done."

Villard's confidence in experimentation in the period of the twenties was perhaps best reflected in his attitude toward the changes occurring in Soviet Russia at the time. On his return from a trip to Russia, where he observed first hand what was taking place there, Villard urged United States recognition of Russia and defended as "wisdom and common sense" allowing the Russians to work out the changes they deemed necessary in their life. "For it is without question," he wrote of the Russian effort, "the greatest human experiment ever undertaken. This, of course, entirely apart from the question whether one believes or does not believe in communism."

But Villard emphatically rejected Soviet methods of implementing the desired changes—methods which he described as those of "savagely crushing their critics or opponents, . . . shooting, imprisoning, and exiling . . . the methods of a Caesar, a Cromwell, a Franz Josef, a Nicholas, and a Mussolini." For the American liberal, however much he desired reform, has been dedicated to the belief that men are sufficiently rational to be able to modify their social institutions in favor of more progressive ones without resort to violence. Positing a need for social reorganization in America after the First World War, Villard made it clear that, as far as he was concerned, the use of force was not the proper means to that end: "We must surely all unite to preach the doctrine that it is utterly wrong to try to upset or alter this government by force . . . . It is a mighty poor American and a stupid, dull reformer who lets himself believe that the way to get a better country is to organize it by bullets or the cowardly infernal machine."

Ten years later, commenting on the crisis resulting from the stock market crash of 1929, Villard said, "Frankly, it seems to me that the time has come for revolt; a peaceful revolution, but none the less revolution." In advocating "peaceful revolution," Villard voiced the liberals' commitment to democratic methods of effecting social changes— a commitment which is the natural consequence of the innate faith and confidence of the American liberal in democratic processes. Villard recognized that the democratic method is a slow one, but he was willing to progress slowly because, he said, "I am still of the opinion that our institutions could be made to work." Thus he rejected far-reaching, comprehensive plans for social change. Writing to former Senator Albert J. Beveridge in 1922, Villard expressed his impatience with those who demanded radical reform: "I am constantly confronted by people who demand a complete program for the future of the coming regeneration of the country. To them, I verily have to reply, that anybody who can do that should be put into the White House at once and that we must grope our way step by step." These same sentiments were to be reflected some ten years later by Franklin D. Roosevelt when he is reported to have exclaimed to his aides, "No blueprints." They represent the liberal technique of adapting a concrete program of action to existing conditions and institutions. It is this perhaps which has led to the oft-repeated criticism that liberals have been without any program of action. Those who make this criticism fail to take into consideration the natural consequences of the pragmatic temper which rejects absolutes.

To the liberal mind, nothing is immune from the therapeutic value of change. The liberal would as soon change the machinery of government as the people who run that

machinery. The American liberal has often been as prone
to recommend changes in the functions of government as
to change his political party. But throughout liberal proposals, the basic assumptions of democracy remain the same,
and the liberal has preferred to work within the framework
of the Constitution. Dedicated thus to both change and constitutional government, the liberal has advocated the orderly
revision of the Constitution as well as a broad construction
of it; dedicated to accomplishing his objectives within
the framework of free institutions, the American liberal
has moved to improve and perfect the machinery of government and to extend political democracy in the direction of
achieving more direct government. Thus he has sought more
responsible and more responsive political institutions.

Viewing the Constitution, President, Congress, and courts
as "tools" in the achievement of social purpose, the American liberal has tended to evaluate them in terms of the results they produce. Villard, in the twenties, found them
all lacking. The Constitution, "originally drawn for a few
struggling newly emancipated Colonies and now applied
to the most powerful and industrially most highly developed
country in the world," was in need of revision: the three
branches of government were to one degree or another ineffective and irresponsible.

Villard's concern over the Presidency was more often
directed at the man than at the office. Generally speaking,
he favored a strong but not all-powerful Executive. His
quarrels with the two Roosevelts, Woodrow Wilson, and
Herbert Hoover were not over the powers they had assumed but over their failure to use the power at their dis-

posal to achieve certain reforms which Villard favored. Of Hoover's failure to recognize Russia, for example, Villard complained, "Man after man comes from the White House and declares privately that he is certain that Mr. Hoover would personally like to recognize Russia, but feels that he cannot because public opinion is not yet ready for it. But for what is a President there except to organize and lead public opinion in the direction in which his conscience tells him to go?"

Because he thought that direct nomination and election of the President and Vice President would strengthen their positions and make them more responsive to the electorate, Villard, throughout the twenties, supported presidential primaries. On the other hand, he urged, with varying degrees of firmness, measures which would make Congress more independent of the Executive. He suggested to Senator George Norris, for example, that a secret ballot in Congress would protect legislators not only from the fanatics on both sides of vital issues, but from the President as well. "I do not believe, for instance," wrote Villard, "that Congress would have put us into the war if there could have been a secret vote to which the President did not have access."

In 1925 Villard had opportunity to congratulate the Senate openly on taking an independent stand against President Calvin Coolidge. The occasion was the nomination by the President of Charles B. Warren of Michigan to the position of Attorney General. The Senate twice refused its consent to the appointment because Warren was charged with having defended the actions of his client, the Michigan Sugar Trust, in violating the antitrust laws. Villard commented in the *Nation*, "Nothing, in my judgment, has honored the Senate more than its display of independence in this matter. To see Borah, Johnson, Norris and Mac-Master . . . refusing to obey the crack of the President's whip is to make one wish to throw up one's hat and give three hearty cheers."

Again, with a view to checking the Executive, Villard favored the use of congressional investigating committees, or at least those originating in the Senate. Fresh in his mind, in the spring of 1925, was the Teapot Dome scandal: "One of the most important recent developments, one of the few successful methods of coping with the demoralizing possibilities of the growing bureaucracy, is the institution of the Senate investigating committees. It takes able men to root out corruption as the two Montana Senators did last Spring."

While generally sympathetic to the Presidency, Villard was much more critical of Congress. In a speech early in 1930 before the League for Independent Political Action, he described congressional efforts in one area as follows:

> As for the Congress, it is as much adrift as is the Executive. For fourteen months it has been trying to give birth to a tariff bill and it is still in labor. Parturition has, however, gone quite far enough to make it clear that what is coming to life is an abortive monstrosity which ought to take its place in circus side-shows with the five-legged calfs, bulls with two heads, and other complete abnormalities.

Of the two Chambers, Villard found the Senate the more responsible. The House he regarded as having sunk almost into obscurity. "No Washington correspondent," he wrote, "goes to its press gallery save on rare occasions; the representatives of the press associations alone attend regularly; its proceedings figure little in the press; it contains only a few men with national reputations."

The reasons, to Villard's mind, for this decline of the House were threefold: its rules limiting debate; the fact that a majority steering committee guided parliamentary procedure, thus expediting the adoption of special rules to favor particular legislation; and the factors surrounding the election of Representatives. Of these causes, the latter seemed to him to be the most significant.

The fact that a member of the House is elected from a single-member district and is traditionally a resident of the district which he represents, coupled with the practice of gerrymandering, Villard pointed out, had resulted not only in considerable localism in American politics but in control of districts by bosses and machines. In comparing the American system of government with that of Great Britain, he remarked that "the advantages are plainly largely, if not wholly, on the side of the British system. Thus the intending candidate for Parliament does not have to stand in the district in which he lives . . . He does not have to go hat in hand to a party boss for permission to run." In answer to the argument that party discipline and loyalty are necessary to responsible government, Villard's only reply was that "it would seem as if the choice were between party regularity [as practiced in the United States] and legislative inefficiency and mediocrity." In contemplating congressional reform, Villard once stated that "so far as Congress is concerned, I should insist upon the seating of the Cabinet upon the floor of the Congress, and I should make it possible for a man of ability to run for Congress in any district, and not necessarily in the district in which he was a resident."

Other aspects of representation in the House of Representatives were publicly aired in the controversy over the seating of Socialist Victor Berger in 1919, 1920, and 1922—a matter which elicited a storm of protest from Villard and his *Nation*. Villard was critical of what he considered the imposition by the House of extraconstitutional qualifications for membership, an imposition which resulted in a denial of the Representative of their choice to the people of Berger's congressional district.

With the exception of Eugene Debs, Victor Berger was the most prominent person convicted under the Espionage Act of 1917. Berger, editor of the Milwaukee *Leader*, was a founder of the Socialist Party in the United States and was its first member to be elected to Congress (1911–13). Berger was a pacifist in the sense that he was opposed to war except in the case of actual invasion. He was a signatory to the Socialist Party's Proclamation and War Program of April 14, 1917, which branded the declaration of war as a crime against the people of the United States and the nations of the world and stated that in all modern history there had been no war more unjustifiable. In pursuance of the Socialist Party's platform declaration calling for continuous, active, and public opposition to the war, Berger, through editorials, articles, and cartoons in the *Leader*, denounced the war policies of the government.

In September of 1917 the *Leader* was deprived of its second-class mailing privilege by the Postmaster General, and in February of 1918 Berger was indicted for conspiracy under the Espionage Act. The following November, still awaiting trial, Berger was elected to the House of Representatives from Wisconsin's Fifth Congressional District. A month later, he was found guilty of sedition and disloyalty and sentenced to twenty years in prison, the maximum sentence under the Espionage Act, by Judge Kenesaw Mountain Landis. Berger appealed his case and was released on bail. Thus he was able to appear in the House in the spring of 1919 to take his seat. His qualifications for membership, however, were challenged, and the question was referred to a special committee under the chairmanship of Representative Frederick W. Dallinger (Republican of Massachusetts). This committee subsequently reported against seating Berger, and the House adopted its report, necessitating a special election in Wisconsin the following December to fill the vacancy. The voters of Milwaukee returned Victor Berger to the House. Once again, in January of 1920, the House refused to seat him. It was not until he had been elected a third time that Berger was allowed to assume his seat. This was in 1922, and there was not a single dissenting vote. In the meantime, however, the Supreme Court had set aside his conviction and sentence under the Espionage Act on the ground of prejudicial conduct on the part of the judge, and the Department of Justice had dropped the espionage charges against him.

Villard fought his battle for Berger on two counts: first, on the matter of what constituted disloyalty, and Villard did not believe Berger had been disloyal; second, on the question of whether or not Congress had the right to refuse Berger his seat and the dangers to our institutions implicit in such a power.

In writing to Representative Frederick W. Dallinger, on July 19, 1919, Villard remonstrated:

May I say to you how disastrous I think it would be if Victor Berger should be disqualified for his seat in Congress on the strength of his conviction in Chicago. If the House of Representatives is going to lay down the rule that it shall pass upon the individual qualifications aside from the election of men sent to Congress, there is going to be established a most dangerous precedent which will go far towards undermining our institutions and add greatly to the tremendous unrest of the country.

Villard was convinced that this denial to a people of their chosen Representative could be duplicated in no other country. "Even the King of Bavaria," he reminded Dallinger, "let Kurt Eisner out of prison when he became a candidate for the Reichstag."

Villard's anger rose in the following months, and in December of 1919, just before the special election in which Berger was returned to the House, the *New York Times* reported that Villard was ready for action. He was urging through the columns of the Socialist daily, the *Leader*, that if Berger was returned and Congress again refused to seat him, the followers of Berger should march on Washington and stage a demonstration at the White House. Villard's purpose was to make a national issue of the case and to rally public opinion around the issue of Congress subverting the wish and the right of the voters of Milwaukee to send a Representative of their choice to Washington. Villard, who, the *New York Times* was careful to point out, "declares he is not a Socialist," stated his case: "The question of whether the lawyers of Congress should be permitted deliberately to slap the voters of the Fifth District in the face by depriving them of the right to have their own representative in Congress should be made a national issue. Any attempt to subvert the will of the voters in the Fifth District would find liberty lovers all over the land registering their protest most emphatically."

Berger *was* returned, and Congress *did* reject him a second time; but there is no evidence that the proposed demonstration ever took place. In his own columns in the *Nation*, there was no mention of a demonstration, and Villard couched the issue in somewhat more reserved language:

> Congress has established a most dangerous precedent in barring Mr. Berger because of its dislike of his opinion as to the war and the future constitution of society. If Mr. Berger is again unseated in the face of this vote by his constituents the House of Representatives will have laid down the rule that in a case where no question of fraud or illegal election has arisen it has the right to say what man shall or shall not represent the Fifth Congressional District of Wisconsin . . . Mr. Berger's district knew exactly what kind of man it was electing; it was fully informed of the charges against him and his sentence by the Federal Court. A majority of its voters have chosen him with their eyes open because they like and believe in Victor Berger and what he stands for.

Yet another aspect of representation in Congress that irritated Villard concerned the Negro in the South. Because the South was effectively denying the vote to the Negro through one means or another, not only did the southern Congressman not truly represent the population of his district, but the vote of the southerner who *did* enjoy the privilege was enhanced. The end result was that the strength and power of those who voted in the South was out of proportion to that of the voters in other sections of the country. Speaking out against the disfranchisement of the Negro by the election laws of the South, Villard pointed up the problem:

> The result of this is a most outrageous disproportion in the power of the Southerners who vote for Congressmen in comparison with those who vote elsewhere. Thus, in South Carolina less than 10,000 people elected a Congressmen [*sic*], whereas every New York Congressman represents on an average 67,338 New Yorkers. In California every Congressman speaks for 85,759 voters. The south with its tiny vote is represented in Washington by forty-five Congressmen while all of New England with its much larger vote has only thirty-two.

To Villard this was clearly a violation of the spirit of the apportionment provisions of both Article I of the Constitution and the Fourteenth Amendment. However, it was only one of several violations. Another provision which the House of Representatives itself was clearly guilty of violating, argued Villard in 1928, was that in Article I, section 2, which provides that reapportionment take place every ten years. The only period in American history when reapportionment did not take place was in the twenties. After the 1920 census, Congress had become deadlocked over the mathmatical formula upon which to base the reapportionment. Villard, in September before the 1928 elections, expressed the fear that "the entire election for Congress next November may be invalidated because the House itself has refused to abide by the plain language of the Con-

stitution." The subsequent Reapportionment Act of 1929
was to provide for automatic reapportionment should Congress fail to act in the future.

The Senate, unlike the House, in Villard's view, generally
attracted men of force and ability who commanded public
attention. It was in the Senate, argued Villard, that the only
significant debate took place. The Senate, therefore, was
worth the time and attention of a journalist: "The Senate
is the one place where they get hope and encouragement,
where they can learn, where there is some color, some life,
some vigor, some truth-telling, some hope of substantial
achievement and much independence." It was fear that
limitation of debate in the Senate would destroy that body's
effectiveness that moved Villard to fight vigorously the
plan of Vice President Charles G. Dawes, when he assumed
the presidency of the Senate in 1925, to limit Senate debate.
To Villard's mind, Dawes was proposing to "bridle the
only important debating body in the world that did not
regularly use cloture of debate."

Villard's main criticism of the Senate centered about the
localism which he detected influencing the actions of Senators. In a *Nation* series entitled "My Dear Senator," Villard
took occasion to lecture his senatorial readers on the immorality of localism and its infringement on duty. With
tariffs as his particular shibboleth, Villard asked, "Why is
it that you . . . cannot see that when you are supporting
this protective system you are committing an immoral act;
that it is grossly immoral for a man to lend himself to a
system which is steadily corrupting our political and economic life on the ground that as long as other people are

getting graft his clients are also entitled to it?" Villard rebuked the Senators for considerations of expedience rather
than a concern for constructive legislation and reform. He
exhorted them to become martyrs if necessary for their
cause and their conscience:

> What does it avail a man to save his election and lose his
> soul if there burns within it the desire to strike out on
> new lines and his conscience tells him to do it? Must you
> always let "I dare not" wait upon "I would"? Is there a
> single moral or economic reform recorded in history
> that was not carried through by men who forgot en-
> tirely to ask themselves how far their perilous advocacy
> would get them, who cheerfully had their heads chopped
> off if necessary to advance their causes?

Henry Steele Commager, in discussing the contributions
of outstanding American liberals from the Populists to
Franklin D. Roosevelt, argues that the acid test of their
pragmatism was their commonly shared "attitude toward
that symbol of traditionalism, the judiciary. As they looked
upon the Constitution as a tool rather than a symbol, so
they regarded the court not as a Delphic Oracle but as a
political institution." [2] Certainly the liberals in Congress
in the twenties—Borah, Norris, La Follette, and Wheeler,
to name a representative few—were in accord with that
view, as was Oswald Garrison Villard.

During the twenties the federal judiciary was under-

[2] Henry Steele Commager, *The American Mind* (New
Haven: Yale University Press, 1950), p. 337.

going a period of conservatism. In a series of decisions handed down between 1917 and 1927, the Supreme Court declared among other things that the federal Child Labor Law was unconstitutional; stock dividends were not income; the Clayton Act did not prevent the use of injunctions in labor disputes; an Arizona law prohibiting injunctions was unconstitutional, the District of Columbia minimum-wage-for-women law was unconstitutional; and the New York criminal anarchy and California criminal syndicalist laws were valid.

Leading liberals fought this conservatism on the ground that the court was employing its prerogative of judicial review to exalt property rights at the expense of human rights.

When President Calvin Coolidge in August of 1927 declared that he did not care to run for re-election, he unwittingly brought on an avalanche of open criticism of the Court. The Coolidge statement led to the usual speculation about whom the Republicans would then select to be their presidential nominee. The name of Charles Evans Hughes was mentioned widely in the press, much to the distress of many liberals who feared the extent to which Hughes carried his belief in the protection of property rights. Villard's *Nation* related:

The Washington newspaper correspondents testified to his accessibility, to the extraordinary lucidity and ability with which he expounded his ideas—and the skill with which he overwhelmed those who dared to doubt the completeness and the correctness of his creed that the sacred right of private property is the foundation of the family and the family the cornerstone of the state.

Villard was particularly worried about the impact the
election of Hughes to the Presidency would have on a
federal court which he felt had already assumed more than
its rightful power. He warned his readers that if Hughes
were elected President "there would be . . . no raising of
the issue as to whether the courts or the people rule this
country."

Three years later Villard was to be among those who
attempted unsuccessfully to defeat the appointment of
Hughes to the Chief Justiceship of the Supreme Court.
Meanwhile Villard charged that the Court harbored judges
who were the "creatures" of corporate wealth. The Court,
far from being the responsible public agency it was designed to be, was, in Villard's view, being manipulated by
special interests.

The Court was also attacked during this period on the
ground that it was usurping through judicial review the
legislative function of deciding which social legislation
was desirable and which was undesirable. Villard commented on this aspect of the matter in a letter to former
Senator Albert J. Beveridge of Indiana as early as 1922:
"The extension of the righteous function of the judge into
other fields is naturally producing a bitter attack, and I
feel very strongly that our judges have got to get back
to the law as it is expounded in England." Liberal criticism
of the Court during the twenties was primarily directed at
a Court which the liberals felt was being used for private
rather than public purposes. Their solution was twofold:
a constitutional amendment giving Congress the power to
override a Supreme Court decision, and the direct election
of federal judges for limited terms. These proposals were
among the platform pledges of Robert M. La Follette in the

presidential campaign of 1924 and were endorsed by Villard as he actively campaigned for La Follette.

Like that of the Progressives before him, Villard's concern over government did not begin and end at the national level but extended to state and local government as well.

The twenties was a period in which the principle of civil service was gradually being adopted at the state and local level of government, and Villard saw in its extension a means of getting better government. Villard was insistent that "here is a reform of the utmost importance which few people understand, the lack of which is in amazingly large degree responsible for the inefficiency and the corruption of Amerian Government." He argued that it ought to permeate all levels of the governmental structure: "The extension of the merit system to cover at least 98% of the offices in any political unit, whether municipal, State or national, would enormously tone up and purify our whole life, and at one blow place us on even terms with the other modern countries of the world." In Villard's view, a basic ingredient of good government was "good" men. He meant "good" in the moral sense, and his was a never-ending hope for such a quality in political office. The twenties, however, brought him some disillusionment with the old reform program of changing the men instead of the fundamental conditions:

I have often been accused of yielding to misguided enthusiasm for public men and believing that in this one or in that one a political savior was at hand, and I must plead guilty to the charge until Woodrow Wilson and

Ramsay MacDonald cured me of that habit. Probably I did stress too much getting a "good man" into high office rather than changing the fundamental conditions. That was partly because McKinley proved how easy it was for a foolish, weak, or unfaithful man in the White House to alter all by himself the whole policy of the country. Moreover, it takes many years to alter fundamental economic conditions or the governmental structure, so one always hopes for a short cut.[3]

In spite of his claim to being "cured" of the belief that *men* were the chief cause of the failure of governmental institutions, Villard never wholly relinquished that view. He never stopped pleading for better men in government. In reiterating his faith in democracy and the workability of American institutions in 1932, Villard maintained that "the fault, in my judgment, has been less with the economic and political system under which we have lived than with the men that we have chosen to work it." At about that same time but on a separate occasion, Villard said, "I am still of the opinion that our institutions could be made to work if the men we entrust with their management had only intellectual honesty, some shreds of political decency, some real patriotism and courage, and some understanding of what is going on in the world." Idealistic though Villard may have been in wanting men of morals to rule, it is obvious that he was realistic enough to observe that angels had not yet assumed command.

On the municipal level, Villard was enthusiastic over the city manager plan which would make the job of the municipal executive a "scientific" or "professional" one and

[3] Villard, *Fighting Years*, p. 183.

thus remove it from political control. He felt, like many other reformers of his day, that the problem of ineffective government could be met in part with new institutions. Villard's hopes for what the city manager plan would accomplish were expressed in a speech at Waterbury, New York, on December 4, 1932:

Our problem in America therefore boils down to this: How can we rescue our cities from the corruption and inefficiency in which most of them wallow, and turn over our municipalities to genuine experts free from all political influence, and yet at the same time maintain the democratic form of government? . . . most of us feel that it is possible to retain the forms of democracy in full vigor, and yet obtain the expert non-partisan honest and efficient leadership which we all crave. The task is, of course, not beyond the abilities of Americans.

Thus Villard reflected well the liberal acceptance of change, experimentation, and faith in the democratic process.

While the attempt to achieve more responsible public officials and institutions has characterized American liberalism, so too has an effort to achieve more responsive institutions. American liberals have persistently sought practical devices by which to maximize the consent of the governed. Striving to extend popular control over public officials, they have fought for the initiative, referendum, recall, and direct nomination and popular election of the President and members of the Senate. The extension of democracy through wider participation of the electorate has been the primary objective; but some, like Villard, believed these procedures would also add protection against abuses in the democratic system. "The best cure for the evils of democracy," argued Villard, "is not less democracy, but more of it." He saw in the extension of democracy through such measures an additional means for keeping the state the servant rather than the master of the people. Villard was reflecting the liberal belief that consensus is possible and that reliance on that consensus obviates government by coercion. He argued that by granting these additional procedures through which the people could assume a greater share in governing themselves they would be rendered less prone to turn "to some totally new system, perhaps to Communism itself." Villard, whose views generally presented as great an antithesis as could be found to those of William Randolph Hearst, was in accord with Hearst on the desirability of the initiative, referendum, recall, and direct primaries. For Villard these were among the few good things Hearst stood for and for which Villard was willing to pay tribute, but he could not resist charging that in Hearst they were "all tarnished by self-interest, by self-seeking."

Writing in June of 1920, the initiative, referendum, and presidential primary were among the "ghosts" of ideals which Villard predicted would be present at the forthcoming Democratic National Convention in San Francisco. By 1927, the reform in question had still not been achieved. "Where are the causes that Woodrow Wilson and Theodore Roosevelt championed in 1912 and until we went into the war," inquired Villard? "There lie promises unfulfilled, a program shattered; a new way of life unchampioned today, yes, forgotten . . . Who speaks now of the referendum, recall, and initiative . . . Who demands that the people shall master their government?"

These liberal efforts to extend political democracy are rooted deeply in the liberal faith in the judgment of average people and their ability to govern themselves—a faith the wellspring of which are the humanism, individualism, and rationalism which contribute to the philosophic basis of the American liberal spirit. Indeed, Louis Hartz has characterized these efforts as being based on the liberal tenet of equalitarianism:

> Why smash bosses and elect senators directly? Why get rid of Croker and Quay? The answer was: to give every last individual an equal chance to govern, and if you throw in the initiative, referendum, recall, and long ballot, to give him a chance to govern in practically every situation. Here was the equity of the Alger world flowering into politics.[4]

[4] Louis Hartz, *The Liberal Tradition in America* (New York: Harcourt, Brace & Co., 1955), p. 240.

CHAPTER VI

Quest for a Liberal Party

THE DESIRE OF the liberals for more responsive and more responsible governmental institutions led to efforts to achieve more "direct" government as well as to their advocating changes in existing governmental institutions. Liberals like Oswald Garrison Villard, however, were not content with these efforts alone. They evidenced concern for the omitted third dimension of Madison's well-worn statement that "in framing a government which is to be administered by men over men, the great difficulty lies in this: you must first enable the government to control the governed; and in the next place oblige it to control itself."[1] American liberals have thus recognized that political power could be abused in spite of internal checks and balances. Forces outside of government, they concluded, must be brought into play to control the government. External restraints were necessary to guide the use, as well as to check the abuse, of political power.

It was the voluntary citizen organization that many liberals accepted as the most efficacious external device for influencing government. The voluntary organizations pro-

[1] *The Federalist* (New York: Modern Library, Inc.), No. 51, p. 337.

vided a medium for the expression of opposition to or support of public policy. They provided a means through which a minority could participate in community affairs, thus rendering them some protection against arbitrary acts of the majority. They represented a medium apart from the vote through which the civic-minded citizen could participate in and influence public affairs.

That Oswald Garrison Villard had confidence in the efficacy of voluntary organizations is attested by the long list of groups to which he belonged over the years. In many, he held office. Among them—and it is not claimed that the list is exhaustive—were the following:

Alien Registration Committee
American Civil Liberties Union
American League to Limit Armaments
American Society for Promoting Efficiency in Every
    Activity of Man
American Union against Militarism
Anti-Imperialist League
Church Peace Union
Citizen's Committee of One Hundred on Behalf of Pull-
    man Porters and Maids
Committee for a State Police
Committee of One Hundred on Ireland
Committee on Militarism in Education
Council against Intolerance in America (Villard resigned
    early in 1940 because of the council's position on
    Charles Lindbergh and Senator Gerald P. Nye. Villard
    was convinced that the charges of anti-Semitism against
    them were unfounded.)
Democratic League of New York

Emergency Committee for Striker's Relief

Friends of Freedom for India

Germanistic Society (Villard resigned from the society
because it would not protest Nazi activities in Germany.)

Haiti–Santo Domingo Independence Society

Keep America Out of War Congress

League for Independent Political Action

Men's League for Woman's Suffrage

National Association for the Advancement of Colored
People

National Committee Against Payment of the Bonus

National Peace Conference

New York Peace Society

New York Progressive Party

People's Lobby to Fight for the People

Postwar World Council

Sacco-Vanzetti National League

Society of Political Science in the City of New York

Special Committee for Protection of the Foreign-Born

The Urban League

Women's International League for Peace and Freedom

In short, Villard could be depended upon for support of
almost any association which he considered in the interest
of reform. Indeed, writing in 1920 in defense of the Committee of One Hundred on Ireland which he had inspired,
Villard argued that citizens have an obligation to take a
hand in public affairs, even international ones, if the government should renege. "I have admitted all along," he said,
"that our procedure was unconventional and bound to attract criticism because of that fact, but the outstanding

thing in the world today is that the governments are the enemies of their peoples and that if the governments will not take a hand in working out international problems, citizens must, or at least should make the attempt."

Voluntary organizations then, in the view of many liberals, were devices for ensuring opposition and minority participation and for influencing public action. As a medium of informed and organized protest and influence, the political party emerged as the most important.

The two-party system in the United States has become an essential mechanism in minimizing the principle of separation of powers, thus helping to achieve political responsibility. The two major parties have become the primary media through which political issues are defined and the choice between alternatives sharpened. In the 1920's however, there seemed reason to believe that the two major parties had failed to fulfill these functions adequately.

Writing in 1919, Villard called attention to the problem of the similarity of the Republican and Democratic parties, charged that they offered no alternative to the people, warned that a movement to the left was on its way in the United States, and called for a new liberal party which would stake out the middle ground between conservatism and socialism:

We must likewise not overlook the truth that our two great political parties are today the most conservative parties in the western world, and that they are even further to the right than the professed British Tories. There is, therefore, no political alternative for those whose desires are unexpressed than to go to the Socialists. If we undertake to organize wisely . . . we shall lend

all possible aid to a liberal party which shall take middle
ground, else shall we see the cleft and the bitter feeling
of the hour grow . . . . One thing is certain, the movement to the left in America is coming.

In 1922 Villard was still protesting, this time to Senator
William M. Calder (Republican, New York): "Now the
only thing for you Republicans and Democrats to do is
to fuse and leave us liberals who are through with both
old parties and want to bring the United States up-to-date
free to form the second party. We are now politically
fifty years behind any modern country." In 1927 Villard
saw so little fundamental difference in the two major parties
that there seemed to be no issues between them. The most
important question of the 1928 campaign, it seemed to him
at the time, would be whether or not the country would
have a "Catholic or a Protestant, a Wet or a Dry." Throughout the presidential campaign of 1932, Villard ran a series
of articles in the *Nation* titled "The Pot and the Kettle."
Their content was for the most part a continuation of a
theme now familiar to his followers: "The pity of it all
is that at bottom it is only the pot attacking the kettle, and
the kettle attacking the pot, and that fundamentally, as I
have said before, the American people are not going to
gain by a change." Of the major-party candidates of the
1932 presidential election, Villard maintained, "Our self-
respect will not permit us to vote for either," and he urged
his readers to cast their vote for Socialist Norman Thomas.
In so doing, however, Villard had no intention of adopting
the Socialist Party, as the party embodying his political
ideals and his hopes for the future. When Villard cast his
vote for Norman Thomas, preferring as he said to be

"dubbed a crank, an impractical idealist, than vote for F.D.R.," he did so for two reasons: first, because of the character of Norman Thomas who, Villard claimed, was "just about the only sincere and politically honest, and unselfish and outspoken political leader on the horizon"; and second, because he conceived of his vote as a protest, in sharp contrast to "throwing it away" on either Hoover or Roosevelt. Villard quoted Norman Thomas: "The only way to throw your vote away is to cast it for somebody you don't really want, and then get him." Villard argued that a large enough protest vote would jolt the Republican and Democratic parties out of their lethargy and at the same time would stimulate the liberal party movement which was very close to his heart:

> A vote for Norman Thomas means another vote of pro-
> test, another serving of notice that the voter is through
> with the old parties; that he wants something different,
> some promise that there will be a genuine attempt to re-
> build our social and political system in a way really to re-
> turn the government to the people . . . One of the fore-
> most practical Democratic politicians in the East has gone
> on record as saying that there will be at least three million
> votes for Norman Thomas in November. If that is the
> case, it will be a protest vote which will make both the
> old parties sit up and take notice, and encourage those
> who desire a third liberal party without the Socialist
> name.

While Villard was insistent throughout the twenties in urging a liberal party, he was also persistent in main-taining that the Socialist Party was not the solution—this

attitude despite his warm and close friendship with Norman
Thomas. Indeed, the liberal party Villard had in mind was
intended to be a compromise. Believing a swing to the left
to be inevitable, he envisioned a party which would meet
the challenge yet not go to the Socialist extreme. The war
years had tended to crystallize Villard's political views,
and as early as 1919 he attempted to explain his position in
a letter to author Hutchins Hapgood:

> Of course, there has been a great change in me. I do not
> see how anyone could have stood still during the last
> few years who thinks at all. One must have moved either
> to the left or to the right and I have gone to the left;
> not so far as you I fancy. I cannot embrace either the
> Socialist or the Communist doctrine . . . . Perhaps I am
> too well off or too happily situated in life—perhaps I
> haven't been close enough to the working people.

Villard was opposed to the Socialist Party on a number of
counts. He was, first, averse to any party which would be
strictly a one-class party. He rejected it, secondly, on the
purely pragmatic ground that it stood no possible chance
of success in the United States because its name was so
discredited:

> I am not interested in the Socialist Party as such, I have
> never joined it nor ever wanted to . . . I consider So-
> cialism to be inevitable and that we are all more or less
> Socialists, even the conservatives. I am willing to grant
> that I found nearly everything in the last Socialist plat-
> form satisfactory to me, but I am nevertheless firmly of
> the belief that no party can get ahead in America under
> the name Socialist.

Last, and most important, Villard simply could not accept the entire Socialist platform. "I am, therefore," he continued, "only interested in starting a new Third Party which may have as a matter of course at least three quarters of the aims of the Socialist Party, but which will be free from the Marxian stamp. I believe that such a party is underway and I sincerely hope that the Socialist organization will become part of it." While willing to agree to public ownership of utilities and natural resources, Villard could not embrace the more comprehensive Socialist doctrine of "social ownership of those things necessary for the common life." The difference between them, he explained to Socialists, was one of degree; and inasmuch as the Socialists could not hope to accomplish anything concrete under the Socialist Party label, Villard felt they could afford to modify their program and join in a movement for a new liberal party:

> So I am very strongly of the hope that we may all get together, now that the socialist party has changed its constitution, and form a new liberal party in which we shall be able to agree upon certain fundamentals in the warfare upon privilege. Our platforms are not so far apart. You came to ours in the La Follette campaign, and many of us, even those who were driven by Mr. Hoover to vote for Mr. Smith, found ourselves in practically complete sympathy with the Thomas platform. You have produced the best leader that there is today in the liberal movement. I cannot see why we should not unite.

A persistent attempt was made throughout the twenties to form a liberal party such as that envisioned by Villard.

In his efforts in that direction he was in the company of liberals such as John Dewey, Paul Douglas, Robert La Follette, Burton K. Wheeler, and others. As early as 1918 and before the end of the First World War, Villard's *Nation* had begun to agitate for a new third party:

> But if there might now arise, even while the war is going on, a united labor party of industrial workers, intellectual workers, and farmers, the vast body of American sentiment which earnestly desires a better political and economic life than that which we are now living would unquestionably have found a programme and a voice.

The third-party movement throughout the period under study tended to assume the possibility Villard voiced above of a farmer-labor alliance which would become permanent. By 1922, however, there seemed to be some basis for these hopes. A National Labor Party had been born in November, 1919, at Chicago. In 1920 this became the Farmer-Labor Party and had some success, particularly in Minnesota. In 1922, and again in a special election in 1923, the Farmer-Labor Party of Minnesota sent representatives to the United States Senate. This undoubtedly gave hope and comfort to those who envisioned a great new party built on a farmer-labor alliance.

In addition, the first Conference for Progressive Political Action had taken place in Chicago in February of 1922. This brought together for the first time labor, farmers, and Progressives. The Railroad Brotherhoods, Socialist and Farmer-Labor parties, the Nonpartisan League, the Committee of Forty-Eight, and various other organizations were represented. Those present at the conference agreed to campaign actively in the November, 1922, election on behalf of candidates who seemed to meet liberal standards and to convene again in December after the elections to assess the results.

There is among the Villard papers a document which is interesting for the light it throws on Senator William E. Borah's interest in a third-party movement. Senator Borah apparently gave serious thought to participating in a new third party. On July 22, 1922, Villard wrote to Ralph Beacon Strassburger, a wealthy Republican, in part as follows:

> I spent last evening with him [Borah] in Washington and found that he is convinced that the only hope is the formation of a new party. He is ready to cut loose as soon as the sinews of war can be organized and the plan laid out . . . . I may say confidentially to you that a strong group of Democrats has offered Borah the Democratic nomination if he would change his seat, but he feels what is true, that the two old parties are so dead that there is no hope of resurrection . . . . We are going to start something in New York this fall, and I am seriously considering running for United States Senator, not with the slightest expectation, of course, that I could be elected, but in order to make a beginning. If we made any kind of a showing the thing might rapidly spread all over the country. Borah thinks that if the means were provided we could organize the entire country in thirty days' time.

Even though Villard may have been overstating Borah's enthusiasm for a new party, it would seem that Borah was closer to lending aid to such a movement than is generally believed to be the case. Borah's biographer, Claudius Johnson, passes rather lightly over Borah's connections with the third-party movement. He relates only that Borah "said the Republicans had to change their program or there would be a third party. During 1923 he had considerable correspondence with J. A. H. Hopkins, chairman of 'The Committee of Forty-Eight functioning as the Liberal Party.' This Committee wanted to draft Borah for their presidential candidate, but he gave them little encouragement." [2] Villard's letter to Strassburger, however, suggests that Villard and his *Nation* had had some indication from Borah personally that he might lend himself to the third-party movement when they continued to press for his leadership throughout 1922, 1923, and even the early part of 1924.

In a letter to Ramsay MacDonald, leader of Britain's Labour Party, dated August 4, 1922, Villard further revealed that he, Villard, was being urged to run for United States Senator on a Labor-Socialist-Farmer Alliance ticket. This was to be the "beginning" to which Villard had referred in his letter to Strassburger, and which, it was hoped, would spread throughout the country.

Villard, however, was not confident that he really wanted to run for public office. On the one hand, he was inclined to "stick to his last"; on the other, he felt that if someone else could not be found to run who could maintain some sort of public standard he would feel duty-bound to do so. A further consideration was the effect his political ventures might have on the standing of the *Nation*, which, historically, was a nonpartisan organ. It was in this vein that he wrote to his friend William Allen White for advice. White replied:

[2] Claudius Johnson, *Borah of Idaho* (New York: Longmans, Green & Co., Inc., 1936), pp. 299–300.

Now about your running for office. I feel that every editor of whatever station should take monastic vows against running for office, no matter how humble the candidacy may be. If you run you sacrifice your influence because some people, inevitably many people—perhaps dull people—but still people capable of influencing public sentiment, if only numerically, will think you want the job and once you lose your virtue, even by specious appearance, you are discredited ever after.

We editors are comparatively few in number, compared with the bulk of the population. "We are feeble yet we build among rocks." There are plenty of people in the world without crippling our editors.

Villard had occasion, two years later, to remind editor White of his advice. In 1924 William Allen White ran for Governor of the state of Kansas on an independent ticket. He was defeated. In conveying his regrets to White over the defeat, Villard commented on White's earlier advice: "I felt then that there are exceptions to all rules; that times may come when even an editor must enter the political lists if he would retain his self-respect and now you have proved me right." Although Villard did not wholeheartedly accept Mr. White's advice, neither did he run for the Senate in 1922 or any other year.

Senator Borah, too, offered Villard advice on his possible candidacy for public office in 1922:

One thing about your personal matter that seems very clear to me and that is if you get into the race it should be under circumstances as to dispel the idea that you are running as a candidate of a group or class. I feel that when

one is nominated on what is called a labor ticket, or a
business man's ticket, or anything of that kind, it is more
or less a challenge to everybody who is not a member of
that particular group and it is a fearful handicap. That
feature of it I think you ought to think over very care-
fully.

It may well be that Borah wanted no large groups alienated
from any movement which he might subsequently lead.

At the same time that Villard was exchanging correspondence on the matter of his own political availability, his *Nation* called upon Senator Borah to lead a new third party.
The *Literary Digest* described the *Nation*'s call as that of
inviting Borah to "rise and be acclaimed as Moses." [3] Borah,
however, never committed himself publicly to the third-
party movement.

The enthusiasm for an effective third party mounted after
the 1922 elections. Candidates endorsed by the Conference
for Progressive Political Action had won in 6 states. Ninety-
three "undesirable" members of the Sixty-seventh Congress
had been defeated, and it was estimated that 140 members of
the new House of Representatives were "progressive-
minded."

Villard was delighted with the outcome of the election.
To him it foreshadowed the future success of the liberal
forces. He wrote Borah, "I wonder if you are as happy as
we are over the election . . . . We are really elated . . .
with the exception of one or two States, the results seem
exactly what we should have wished. It's a magnificent beginning, isn't it?"

A second Conference for Progressive Political Action met

[3] "Borah and a Third Party," *Literary Digest*, LXXIV (August 26, 1922), 14.

in Cleveland, Ohio, the following December. Just prior to its meeting, however, a dinner sponsored by the People's Legislative Service was held in Washington, D.C. This organization had been inspired by Senator Robert La Follette in the spring of 1921 and was launched with the help of Oswald Villard to provide members of Congress and the people with reliable information on matters pending in Congress. It was composed of a group of liberals both within and outside of Congress—men and women like George Norris, Robert La Follette, Burton K. Wheeler, Amos and Gifford Pinchot, Roger Baldwin, Herbert Croly, Jane Addams, and John Haynes Holmes. Oswald Garrison Villard was a member of its Executive Committee. The first Conference for Progressive Political Action had actually grown out of a Washington dinner meeting of this organization. The Service's dinner on the eve of the second conference of the "Progressives" drew the attention of the press and gave the liberals some much-needed publicity along with the prestige value of such names as Norris and La Follette. It helped to stimulate the interest of farm and labor groups in the formation of an independent political organization. The liberal elements of American society seemed now to have gathered enough strength to bid for the Presidency. When a third Conference for Progressive Political Action met in February of 1924, it adopted the following statement of purpose:

> The Conference for Progressive Political Action is an organization created for the purpose of securing the nomination and election of Presidents and Vice Presidents of the Untied [*sic*] States, United States Senators, Representatives to Congress, members of State Legislatures and other state and local public officers who are pledged to

the interests of the producing classes and to the principles of genuine democracy in agriculture, industry and government.[4]

To further its purpose, the Conference for Progressive Political Action decided to hold a national convention in 1924, which would follow, chronologically, that of the Democrats and the Republicans, to decide which political candidates it would support. Such a convention was called for what seemed to the leaders a most appropriate date— July 4, 1924. Finding neither Calvin Coolidge, the Republican nominee, nor John W. Davis, the Democratic candidate, acceptable, the National Committee of the conference announced on the eve of the convention that it had asked Robert M. La Follette to run as its candidate for the Presidency. Villard had been actively seeking La Follette's candidacy for at least five months. On February 1, 1924, he had written to La Follette somewhat flamboyantly:

> I do not know how you can be in any doubt whatever as to your duty in view of what is coming out in the revelations of the Teapot Dome. If you do not give us a chance, by running on a third ticket, to vote for you, hundreds and hundreds of thousands, perhaps millions, of us American citizens will be denied the opportunity to express ourselves at the polls. We are sick and tired of voting for Tweedle-Dum and Tweedle-Dee.

La Follette accepted the invitation and in due course was endorsed by the conference to run for the Presidency as an Independent, postponing until after the election the question

[4] Quoted in Kenneth MacKay, *The Progressive Movement of 1924* (New York: Columbia University Press, 1947), p. 76.

of establishing an actual third party. The selection of the vice-presidential candidate was also postponed. There is some evidence that Villard was considered for the post. The issue was resolved a few days later, however, when Senator Burton K. Wheeler of Montana bolted the Democratic Party on the basis that he could not "support any candidate representing the House of Morgan." He was immediately invited to become La Follette's running mate.

Oswald Garrison Villard publicly proclaimed his approval of these events. In the *Nation*, he described the convention of the Conference for Progressive Political Action as an "honest" one. The esteem with which Villard held that convention body is implicit in his remark that La Follette, in receiving its nomination, had "received the highest compliment which could be paid short of the presidency itself." Villard elaborated:

> The honor was a far greater one than had it come from the Republican or Democratic Party. Here were no political bosses, no ward heelers, no Harry Daughertys, no Tom Taggerts, and no Henry Cabot Lodges—just twelve hundred plain people come together under labor-union auspices to take their stand . . . .
>
> . . . . .
>
> Sincerity, earnestness, honesty—these were the qualities which ruled . . . here was the search for truth which makes man free; here was a refusal to remain longer in bondage to a dead and festering past; here was the ambition to lead and to find new ways to serve.

Villard became an energetic and loyal campaigner for La Follette in 1924. In a letter to La Follette on July 11 of that year, he pledged his personal support. "Please do not

forget," he wrote, "that I am ready to devote my time from
the 15th of September until election day to your cause, without compensation, and insofar as possible I shall defray my
own expenses in case you call upon me for any speaking."
Just three days after Senator Wheeler agreed to be La
Follette's running mate, the *New York Times* reported that
Villard was chairman of a committee of one hundred liberal
professional and business men and women combined in support of La Follette. The committee was composed of liberals
such as Norman Hapgood, John Haynes Holmes, Arthur
Garfield Hays, Robert Morss Lovett, Amos Pinchot, and
Norman Thomas. They wired La Follette an expression of
their gratitude to him for his willingness to assume leadership and pledged their votes and efforts in aid of his candidacy. On July 28 Villard wrote to La Follette pledging the
financial support of the *Nation*. "We of the Nation," he informed La Follette, "have decided to open our own fund
for your candidacy and appeal to our readers for gifts. The
office force on the spot has contributed $250."

A month later, on August 23 and 24, the National Executive Committee of the La Follette–Wheeler Campaign met
in a planning session. Villard was present and was appointed
a committee of one to arrange a banquet to be held on September 15 at Madison Square Garden. He was also named
to a committee charged with securing a financial director
for the campaign. Subsequently, he became Assistant National Treasurer of the so-called "Progressives." He toured
New York State with Burton K. Wheeler, acting—as he describes it—"as a curtain-raiser" for the vice-presidential candidate. He then went on to tour the United States on behalf
of La Follette and Wheeler.

Villard was not, however, completely happy with the

issues which La Follette chose to stress in his campaign. While La Follette seemed preoccupied with domestic issues, Villard kept pressing him to deal with foreign affairs and to speak out against war. He urged La Follette repeatedly to give more attention to Negro votes as a source of strength —to speak out, for example, on the Haiti and Santo Domingo issues. In short, La Follette's program, as Villard described it some years later, was never "thorough-going" enough:

> He was against privilege but he failed to see that the tariff is the greatest bulwark and creator of privilege; he opposed corruption but he voted regularly for the tariff system which for generations gave rise to more political corruption than anything else. He was opposed to war but he was not a pacifist—he could not see that he who compromises with this evil and refuses to break with it at all times, under all conditions, merely helps to continue it, helps it more than does the outright advocate of war. He believed in co-operation yet lacked the vision to see what enormous benefits the whole country would derive if it were made of paramount importance.

At the time of the 1924 campaign, however, Villard was convinced that the campaign marked the resurgence of American liberalism. It had, he wrote, "revived hope, re-inspired faith that political progress is not dead, that leaders can be found to assail the massed forces of wealth and privilege even as at different times and in different ways they have been challenged by Theodore Roosevelt and Woodrow Wilson."

The results of the 1924 campaign are well known and need no elaboration here. Suffice it to emphasize that when

4,822,319 votes were cast for La Follette that November 4, more votes were cast for a minor-party organization than in any other election in American history. The "Progressives" carried only Wisconsin, but they relegated the Democrats to third place in eleven other states (all west of the Mississippi). Significant also is the fact that this election marked the first formal alliance in the United States of organized labor with farmers and Socialists.

Villard was, of course, bitterly disappointed in the outcome of the election. He attributed the failure of the liberal forces to a variety of causes. Villard charged first that management of the campaign was inefficient: Gilbert Roe, director of the New York headquarters, "was not a good administrator and did not know people in New York"; La Follette had a tendency "to put trusted men in charge without the slightest reference to their effectiveness"; and Villard himself was scheduled to speak in small towns where he was not known instead of in large cities where he had standing as a liberal leader.

Second, Villard cited organizational weaknesses and financial difficulties as obstacles to a successful campaign. He charged that "in many places we found the merest skeletons of what a fighting political force should be, and in some States we had no organization whatever and could not get on the ballot." [5] He expanded upon this latter point and campaign finances in a letter to Britain's Prime Minister, Ramsay MacDonald:

. . . In one State we were entirely barred, and in California we could only be represented through the Socialist ticket which kept several hundred thousand people from

[5] Villard, *Fighting Years*, p. 503.

voting for us . . . . We only succeeded in raising about $230,000, and being without organization and with precious few leaders we had to struggle against incredible odds. We only had seventeen national speakers in the field until October, of whom I was one, and some of us had even to pay our own expenses. Under the circumstances victory was unterrly [*sic*] impossible.

Third, Villard blamed the ambivalence of labor for the defeat. He relates in his *Fighting Years* that the American Federation of Labor had promised its support and $3,000,000 of its funds. Actually, the total receipts from all sources amounted to only $221,837. The New York Labor Council, which had earlier endorsed La Follette, withdrew its support in the last days of the campaign. Villard cited the attitude of labor as one of the problems involved both in the campaign and in attempting to build a permanent Progressive organization after the election:

What we are trying to do now is to organize permanently. One of our chief difficulties is the benightedness of the labor unions. Gompers has gone back to his old position of antagonism to a labor party, and while he is not likely to last much longer most of his entourage is of the same point of view. Their following was not always sincere in its support of us, and many of the New York unions deliberately sold us out in the last week of the campaign, presumably for cash.

Professor John Hicks has reported of the third-party movement of the twenties that with the defeat of La Follette "all plans to develop a permanent organization were abandoned." [6] Strictly speaking, this is not true. There were among the liberal forces some who never completely relinquished the idea of a permanent third-party organization. Villard for one continued to urge such a party and worked toward that end right up to the presidential election of 1932.

The delegates to the Cleveland meetings of the Conference for Progressive Political Action had agreed that there should be a call to a special convention to be held after the November elections of 1924 to consider the question of forming a permanent third party around the La Follette supporters. By the time the convention met late in February of 1925, however, the Railroad Brotherhoods and the American Federation of Labor had already withdrawn their support of the activities of the Conference for Progressive Political Action and had indicated that in their opinion a third-party attempt would be futile. The conference, thus weakened, was adjourned almost as soon as it was called to order, with the provision that those who remained interested in a third-party movement should meet together that night. Those delegates who remained for the evening session declared themselves a "convention of delegates to a new independent political party." [7] An executive committee was named and a national headquarters established. The latter became known as the National Progressive Headquarters of the New Political Party. Oswald Garrison Villard was one of its leaders along with Dr. Mercer Green Johnston of Baltimore, a member of the Committee of Forty-Eight, Arthur Garfield Hays,

[6] John Hicks, "The Third Party Tradition in American Politics," *Mississippi Valley Historical Review*, XX (June, 1933), 3–28.

[7] MacKay, *op. cit.*, p. 236.

and Peter Witt. Not enough interest was shown by liberal groups throughout the country even to call a convention in 1926. Villard and Peter Witt had composed a "Declaration of Progressive Faith" for the national committee which was destined never to be read before a party convention. The national committee continued to meet from time to time, however, and attempts were made to organize liberals in various areas throughout the country. Villard, for example, was quite active throughout 1925 and 1926 in organizing a Progressive Party in New York State. On June 14, 1925, he gave the opening address at the State Convention of the New York Progressive Party in which he stated the objectives of the convention. "We are met together," he said, "not to plan another campaign, not to try to intrigue now as to when we shall next go to the polls with a party . . . But to renew our faith, to take counsel with one another as to how we shall proceed when the political tide begins to turn." [8] The convention was called, he continued, so that the party could keep faith with the 5,000,000 voters who cast ballots for "Progressive" candidates in 1924.

On January 14, 1926, Villard wrote to Gilson Gardner, Scripps-McRae correspondent in Washington, D.C., requesting his aid in gathering together a group of liberal Congressmen for a dinner of the New York Progressives. In explaining his purpose, Villard intimated the difficulty of holding the liberals together:

Our group is quite conscious of the fact that if we do not do something to keep the movement alive it will disintegrate very rapidly. On the other hand the group feels restless because it has not been in touch with the men who

[8] *New York Times*, June 14, 1925, p. 24, col. 4.

led us in the last campaign, and it feels that a visit of this kind at Washington would perhaps stimulate these Progressives by letting them know that there is a group of people in New York who are watching them and ready to support them where they can.

In October of 1927, Villard addressed the Progressive Club of Hampshire County, Massachusetts. Into his address was injected something new for Villard. He indicated that he was ready to settle for something less than a new third party:

> Let me say here that my appeal is for an opposition and that I am not concerning myself at this hour with whether that should come from a splitting up of the two old parties with the subsequent coalescing of similar elements in them both, or in some other way. I believe that it would be best to achieve this result by the rise of a third party . . . But the need of a check upon the dominant party in Washington and the dominant economic forces is so great that I am prepared to welcome it if it could come about by a realignment and a re-birth of one of the existing parties. It is principles with which Progressives everywhere ought to be primarily concerned and not with mediums; fortunately the battle for these principles can be carried on in and out of season, whether there is or is not a party or even a Congressional group committed to them as long as there are pens to write, newspapers to print, and tongues to speak.

This speech foreshadowed the end of the National Progressive Headquarters of the New Political Party. A month

Henry Villard

Brown Brothers

Copyright by Underwood & Underwood, N. Y.
Fanny Garrison Villard

Oswald Garrison Villard (about 1918)

Wide World Photo

Newsmen visiting the site of the Dnieper River hydroelectric project during a tour of Russia in 1929. Left to right, standing: Ernest K. Lindley and Joseph Gollomb; seated, H. V. Kaltenborn, James A. Mills, Col. Hugh Cooper (American engineer), Oswald Garrison Villard.

New York City breadline in the early 1930's.

Delegation appearing in Albany before the Senate and Assembly Codes Committee of the State legislature to appeal for the abolishment of capital punishment in New York State (1930). Among those identified, left to right, standing: Ruth Hale, Oswald Garrison Villard (center), Arthur Garfield Hays, Dudley Field Malone; seated: Dr. Frederick L. Hoffman (center).

Oswald Garrison Villard addressing Western Reserve University
students in a demonstration against war (1935).

Oswald Garrison Villard (standing) and Norman Thomas
(seated, far right) addressing an anti-Hague machine rally at
Princeton University in 1938. Students are John VanEss, Jr.
(seated, left) and J. Harlan Cleveland (seated, right).

Oswald Garrison Villard, representing the Committee on Militarism in Education, testifying before the Senate Military Affairs Committee in opposition to compulsory military education (1940).

later, on November 3, 1927, the motion to adjourn sine die was carried. It also foreshadowed a new emphasis in the activities of the "Progressives." They were subsequently to concentrate on maintaining and enlarging the liberal group within Congress and on a realignment of the old parties. To this latter end, Paul Douglas, John Dewey, and others were instrumental in organizing in 1929 the League for Independent Political Action. This organization was to act as a kind of clearing house for liberal sentiment and ideas, contacting and cooperating with liberals throughout the country and cultivating a sense of solidarity.

Lack of organization has long been regarded as the chief weakness of liberalism. Woodrow Wilson had it in mind when he explained to Franklin D. Roosevelt:

> Roosevelt, we progressives never beat the conservatives because they, wanting to disturb nothing, and maintaining a purely defensive position, have the cohesiveness and resistance of a closed fist; but we, being determined to make progress and each knowing best how it should be done and being therefore utterly unable, any of us, to support any others of us, have about as much striking power as you'd expect from the fingers of an open hand, each pointing in a slightly different direction.[9]

By 1929 the liberals, it would seem, had finally recognized that hastily improvised campaigns in presidential years were not conducive to the establishment of permanent political parties. They had begun to see that their best hope for a

[9] Related by Rexford Tugwell in "The New Deal: The Progressive Tradition," *Western Political Quarterly*, III (September, 1950), 395–96.

permanent third party was to organize from the grass roots upward. John Dewey expressed the realization:

> The hope of the future resides . . . first and foremost in a campaign of steady and continuous organization which shall effect contact and unity among the now scattered and largely inarticulate liberal persons and groups in our country. Secondly, as in part a means for this organized acquaintance and contact and in still greater part as a product of it, the development of a unifying body of principles and policies adapted to present conditions, one which will bring that sense of reality into present politics which is now absent.[10]

That Villard was sympathetic to this approach and acquiesced in it is apparent from an address he gave before the Rollins College Institute of Statesmanship in March of 1929. Positing that a truly liberal party was possible in the United States, he attempted an analysis of the problems involved and argued that the first step was to organize for a far-flung liberal sentiment in the United States:

> Historically in American life new parties arise either around some striking, inspiring personality, or some compelling economic issue, or they have been born out of a profound sectional distress. The difficulty of the situation today is that since the death of the senior Robert M. La Follette, there is no outstanding leader about whom an organization can be built, and there is no single compelling economic issue . . . The difficulty which confronts liber-

[10] John Dewey, "What Do Liberals Want?" *Outlook*, CLIII (October 16, 1929), 261.

als and radicals today is the extraordinary multiplicity of issues and reforms which they would champion . . . But what can be done now without a leader, or a party name, or funds, or a single paramout issue? I answer that the way to begin is to begin; the way to organize is to organize; that the way to fight is to fight, and to fight wherever the opportunity offers, especially locally. There are enough progressives powerfully to affect Congress, at least to send some representatives to it, if they could only come together. Unfortunately, they are often unaware of another's existence, partly because of the reign of reaction since the war, partly because there has been no common ground of association; partly for lack of a personality to rally about.

Villard was suggesting the identical line of attack which the League for Independent Political Action had adopted. May 22, 1931 found him addressing that organization on the occasion of the second anniversary of its founding. He criticized the Democrats for the inadequacy of their opposition and called for a "new deal" in precisely those terms:

> In the face of all this it is more than ever the duty of every far-sighted American to demand a new deal, to make it plain to all to whom he can appeal that there is not an iota of difference between the party of power and the party of opposition . . . What we need above all else today is a party which shall be at least as radical as the Bull Moose of 1912, and the La Follette crusade of 1924.

By September of 1931, however, Villard again expressed little hope of reform through the major parties and was

sounding out Harold Ickes, then a Chicago attorney who
had long been active in the Progressive movement, on
whether or not Ickes would be interested in a new-party
movement which was in its embryo and which had evolved
from the activities of the League for Independent Political
Action:

> I write to inquire whether you would be interested in the
> Third Party movement started here under the leadership
> of John Dewey, with Paul Douglas as one of the Vice-
> Chairmen, and myself as Treasurer. The only thing that
> limits us is the question of money, and under existing con-
> ditions with everybody feeling the pinch it is terribly
> hard to get funds. At the same time, the interest in our
> cause is tremendous . . . we have something like 5,000
> members, and we are planning a preliminary meeting this
> fall and then another more public and important meeting
> next winter.

June of 1932 found Villard still urging a new party. The
Democrats had nominated Franklin Delano Roosevelt as
their presidential candidate, and Villard considered Roosevelt something less than a liberal:

> To put into the Presidency at this hour another weak man
> in the place of Herbert Hoover would be all the more
> disastrous because of the mistaken idea that Franklin D.
> Roosevelt is really a liberal . . . .
>
>   But, we shall be asked again, whom would you have the
> Democrats nominate? This is not our function. We are
> not supporters of the Democratic Party and we have long
> since told our readers that we shall not support a candidate

of either of the old parties. We stand with President
Butler in his belief that the hour calls for a new party and
that nothing less will serve, but unlike President Butler
we are ready to go through with the proposal. We wish
the beginning made here and now.

As the campaign progressed, the ranks of the liberals di-
vided. Men like George Norris, Robert M. La Follette, Jr.,
Burton K. Wheeler, and Frank Walsh of New York sup-
ported Roosevelt. On the other hand, such names as Morris
Ernst, Morris Cohen, Elmer Davis, Paul Douglas, and John
Dewey were found joined with that of Villard in a vote of
protest for Norman Thomas. The latter did not foresee
Roosevelt's New Deal and the subsequent realignment of
American politics into the liberal and conservative group-
ings that Villard in particular had for so long advocated.

The third-party movement of the 1920's may be interpreted as an attempt to unify the scattered fronts of liberalism into a single, continuing force—a force dedicated to
criticism of the *status quo* in a period of rapidly changing
conditions of a technological society. Oswald Garrison Villard was the type of man needed by every such movement
if it is to be successful. An indefatigable committeeman,
willing and able to lavish time and energy behind the scenes,
Villard was inherently optimistic and almost dogmatic in his
confidence that the American people would recognize, and
were ready and willing to accept, able and responsible
leadership.

CHAPTER VII

Repudiation of a "Business" Society

THE PERIOD OF the twenties was one in which liberals appraised capitalist democracy with the aim not of disturbing the effectiveness of capitalism but of reducing the incidence of corruption in governmental relations with business and of emphasizing the fact that the capitalistic system was not a self-operating machine which would run effectively and satisfactorily with little or no governmental supervision.

The decade was marked by an increasingly insistent demand by liberals for governmental action in the economic sphere. This was not a new phenomenon to America. It was characteristic of the agrarian movements of the late 1800's; it was an integral part of the Progressive movement and the New Freedom; it was to culminate eventually in the New Deal. Its roots were in the abuses resulting from the continued rise and concentration of big business. This demand reflected a growing recognition of the economic bases of politics, of the role of wealth and of pressure groups in the political process. It reflected also the liberals' conviction that opposition to unlimited power should apply to the economic as well as to the political arena.

Pressure for economic intervention by government in the twenties was inextricably interwoven with the attempts by liberals to obtain more responsive political institutions. Agitation for a constitutional amendment giving Congress a vote over Supreme Court decisions, for example, was a protest against use of judicial review "to exalt property rights at the expense of human rights." [1] By the same token, the concerted movement for a third party was a protest against the conservatism of both major parties because of their domination by economic interests; in Villard's words, the task of building a third party was vital "unless we are to be permanently enchained by those whom Wilson called the real masters of America, its Big Business men." Moreover, the specific connection between political corruption and economic power became more apparent after the turn of the century, making them related problems and rendering their solution a simultaneous one. To Villard and his liberal friends, it seemed as though the special interests were firmly entrenched in Washington. "It is now," he wrote in 1927, "a government by, for, and of Big Business." And the liberals were insistent that that government be transformed to one devoted to the general interest.

The Republican program of the twenties has often been referred to as a "return to laissez faire." It has also been described as a modified form of mercantilism. Basis for both views is found in statements of the leaders of the Republican Party of the period. Said President Harding, for example, "We want a period in America with less government in Business and more Business in government." Maintained Coolidge, "The business of America is business"; and in Hoover's words, "Hamilton's view well comprehended the necessities of Federal Government activity in support of commerce and industry." Thus there was an ambivalence to

[1] Louis Hacker, *American Problems of Today* (New York: F. S. Crofts and Co., 1938), p. 91.

the Republican acceptance of laissez faire. The "business service" concept of the function of government as put forth by Presidents Harding, Coolidge, and Hoover is more akin to mercantilism. Yet the very same advocates of government aid to business were opposed to most forms of government regulation and control. In this respect, they were expounding more nearly a laissez faire doctrine.

Thus American liberals in the twenties fought their "business civilization" on two fronts. First, they opposed the government's benevolence to business, mainly as it took the form of tariffs and other subsidies. Second, they advocated greater control of business and natural resources by government.

As this chapter develops, it should become apparent that liberal opposition to established economic interests in the twenties was made in the name of individualism. It is the theory of individualism which underlies the liberal insistence on dissolution of monopolies and holding companies. The hope was for restoration of fair competition and its accompanying opportunities. Where government regulation, ownership, and control were advocated, it was in the interest of individual dignity, freedom, and opportunity. Indeed, the immediate problem was that of method—of how to realize the individualistic, humanitarian, and libertarian tenets of the liberal faith in a world dominated by big business which, seemingly, was frustrating liberal aspirations.

The concentration of private economic wealth and power, for example, left little room for the equal opportunity of individuals to realize their potential. Villard, with reference to Herbert Hoover's philosophy of rugged individualism, described the situation as follows:

Again and again he has made it plain that what he calls the "American system" precisely fulfils his dreams, his aspirations. He admits that there are some flaws, but he dwells upon the superiority of our democracy to the British, German, or French democracy because of the equality of opportunity which he says the United States offers. But that equality of opportunity means for him the right of some men to rise to wealth and power and privilege upon the backs of most of their fellow-citizens. He snorts at the idea that there may be a better system, a better way of life for Americans.

To the American liberal, opportunity for the fullest and freest development was to be accorded all men, humble and obscure as well as great and powerful. Thus the doctrine of individual rights underwent an extension to include the right to a certain amount of economic security. Man needed more than a mere subsistence living to enable him to do the things he really wanted to do, to achieve a meaningful measure of self-realization. He needed liberation from the material insecurity which denied him the opportunity to participate in the vast cultural resources at hand.

Turning to the more strictly humanitarian aspect, the American liberal, as characterized in the twenties by such men as Oswald Garrison Villard and John Dewey, could not tolerate a smug indifference to social evils. Theirs was a keen sense of social responsibility or the "social justice" of the earlier Progressive movement. American liberalism, as Dewey said, was "identified largely with the idea of the use of governmental agencies to remedy evils from which the less-fortunate classes suffer." [2] Its ultimate objective was to alleviate social inequities and to eliminate economic abuses.

It was obvious to the liberals of the 1920's that the Amer-

[2] John Dewey, "A Liberal Speaks Out for Liberalism," *New York Times Magazine*, Feb. 23, 1936, p. 3.

ican free enterprise system had not for some decades realized
the human satisfactions originally expected of it. Depressions,
monopolistic abuses, poverty in the midst of plenty—all
pointed to the failure of the economic system to meet the
needs of modern industrial, economic, and social conditions.

It would seem inevitable that the proper relationship between government and business, between politics and economics, would become the most controversial, crucial, and
central question in American political thought of the twentieth century. It was natural that the role of government
should be re-examined in the light of the realization that economic interests had, either by usurpation or by default of
other segments of society, assumed the function of determining the major objectives of society and the cultural
destinies of mankind.

It was only natural, too, for the pragmatic liberal to conclude that free enterprise had failed and therefore had to be
modified and that this task should be turned over to a political authority controllable by the people. The liberal is on
the side of positive government rather than laissez faire.
Knowing that the exercise of power is unavoidable in modern, industrial society, the basic problem of the liberal involves the question of control of that power. Who should
wield it? And in whose behalf? The American liberal decided the question in favor of collective action through the
medium of a positive state—a state devoted to the wise use of
political power to promote the general welfare. The American liberal accepted the thesis that it was a proper function
of the state to safeguard a considerable measure of social and
economic security for ordinary men. As economic stability
and security became a warranted objective of public policy,
some degree of governmental control and regulation was
necessarily implied.

The precise degree of governmental control and regulation advocated by American liberals, however, has been somewhat nebulous. To begin with, the American liberal has never attempted to change fundamentally the economic system. Rather than replacing that system, he has been concerned with correcting it, with making it work. In seeking, for example, to restore free competition through trust regulation, he has in effect sought to *protect* the free enterprise system. In his preoccupation with the economic welfare of the individual, he has been concerned to see that capitalism should fulfill the promise that it can best provide the fullest and freest benefits to society. The liberal has had no blind devotion to either public or private ownership. He has been pragmatically inclined rather to respect private ownership until experience indicates that abuses or inadequacies require public responsibility in a given case.

The American liberal has suffered the usual vulnerability of the middle ground position. He has been attacked by the right because he insisted on change, by the left because he would not go far enough. Louis Hartz describes the liberal mind as "like that of a child in adolescence, torn between old taboos and new reality." [3] Max Lerner, who was once associated with Oswald Villard on the *Nation* and broke with him over the question of liberal program, criticized Villard by characterizing his position as that of pacifist liberalism which "was a woefully inadequate weapon with which to confront a ruthless and planless corporate capitalism." [4]

But liberals like Oswald Garrison Villard could not be expected to advocate drastic changes in the prevailing economic system. Villard himself was a man of material means

[3] Hartz, *op. cit.*, p. 237.
[4] Max Lerner, *Ideas Are Weapons* (New York: The Viking Press, Inc., 1939), p. 180.

gained through the graces of a capitalistic system. While recognizing the deficiencies of that system, he nevertheless retained a fundamental respect for it. And he observed how that system was being modified in other parts of the world. Villard argued repeatedly that it was his intent to ward off radicalism in the United States by utilizing political power to meet the more immediate economic and social problems of the day:

> One thing is certain, the movement to the left in America is coming. No one can study conditions abroad and rest assured that America can remain apart from the imponderable world currents. . . . Shall we guide it and direct it into wise channels by ascertaining and removing the causes of social and economic discontent, or shall we combat it by force and repression and lynching—and thereby compel it to nihilism and to what people consider bolshevism?

Louis Hartz gives credit to the liberals for their part in making socialism in America impossible: "Actually, though the whole of the national liberal community sent the Marxists into the wilderness, the final step in the process which did so was the nature of American Liberal Reform." [5]

What *was* the nature of the liberal reform? What *were* the measures which Villard and others urged to meet social needs and yet obviate radicalism? What, in effect, constituted the liberal rejection of a "business civilization" and repudiation of laissez faire in the twenties? Tariffs, subsidies, railroads, public power, utilities, natural resources, trusts, and depression measures in the late twenties and early thirties—all figured largely in giving definition and

[5] Hartz, *op. cit.*, p. 233.

concrete expression to the liberal concept of the economic role of government.

One of the hardest fought battles of the Progressive movement of 1908 to 1912 was that over the Payne-Aldrich Tariff Act of 1909. The Republican Party had pledged itself, in the 1908 presidential campaign, to a revision of the tariff, and one of President William Howard Taft's first actions on entering the White House was to call Congress into special session for this purpose. The resulting legislation embraced revision, but a revision upward, much to the disgust and disappointment of liberal Senators such as La Follette of Wisconsin, Borah of Idaho, and Beveridge of Indiana, who had fought it bitterly. In spite of their opposition, the bill was a series of concessions to the demands of numerous special interests.

When Woodrow Wilson assumed the Presidency, he, too, called a special session of Congress following his inauguration to deal with tariff reductions. He recognized that tariffs were a form of privilege and a means of harboring economic inefficiency: "We must abolish everything that bears even the semblance of privilege or of any kind of artificial advantage, and put our businessmen and producers under the stimulation of a constant necessity to be efficient, economical, and enterprising, masters of competitive supremacy, better workers and merchants than any in the world . . . . It is best, indeed it is necessary, to begin with the tariff." [6]

The response to Wilson's plea was the Underwood Tariff Act of 1913, a strictly Democratic measure, which

[6] Shaw, *op. cit.*, I, 8–9.

embraced moderate protection based on the principle of a revenue tariff without injury to business. The Republican principle of equalizing production costs at home with those abroad was abandoned.

With Republicans back in control of government in the twenties, it seemed only natural that businessmen should demand and legislators grant an immediate revision of the Democratic tariff. Indeed, the first act of Congress passed under the Harding administration was the Emergency Tariff Act of May 27, 1921. This legislation was succeeded by the Fordney-McCumber Act of 1922 and, in Herbert Hoover's administration, the Smoot-Hawley Act of 1930. Neither the Fordney-McCumber nor the Smoot-Hawley acts were content to return tariffs to the level of the Payne-Aldrich Act of 1909. Instead, these acts imposed higher tariffs than ever before established in United States history—a circumstance which was anathema to Oswald Garrison Villard. Next in order after the sedition and conscriptive legislation of World War I, he considered the Fordney-McCumber Act the "wickedest piece of legislation ever put through Congress."

Villard, it will be remembered, assumed full editorial control of the *Nation* in January of 1918. In its very first edition of that year, Villard put forth what he called "some reconstruction proposals." One of them called for the establishment of free trade and the abolition of all protective tariffs. "This involves," said Villard, "freedom of the seas and of trade to all peoples of the earth without fear or favor or special or preferential rights of any kind." Fourteen years later he was still advocating free trade. He had found little in the tariff outlook of Presidents Harding, Coolidge, or Hoover in which to take comfort.

Actually, Villard fought the protective tariff all his life and always with a considerable amount of moral indignation, passion, and journalistic fervor.

To Oswald Garrison Villard the tariff was not only economically unsound and politically undemocratic, but it was "wicked"; it was "robbery"; it was "extortion." Villard was uncompromising. Their attitude toward the tariff brought condemnation and public criticism by Villard to Republicans and Democrats, farmers and laborers alike during this period. Of the Republican Party, he said that it was the "party of protection and privilege and wealth"; the Democrats, "forgetting their old slogan of victory, 'a tariff for revenue only,'" were helping to erect additional tariffs; labor had adopted a position of "stupidity" on the tariff; "nor is the situation in the least bit changed," he said, "if other groups, like the farmers, also seek and obtain tariff favors." Villard opposed tariffs on a number of counts.

First, free trade was a necessary prerequisite to peace. Tariffs contributed to war among nations by fostering rivalry, by encouraging "the great illusion" that colonies and spheres of influence were worth fighting for. Tariffs became a manifestation of nationalism gone wild, of imperialism, and of trade following the flag. Tearing down the tariff wall would clear the atmosphere of war and would allow fair and just competition among nations.

Second, establishment of free trade would in turn contribute to the world's postwar financial recuperation. It would allow the smaller nations a fairer chance to rebuild their economies. Tariff reduction, and free trade generally, would, by rendering war less likely, make armaments and the maintenance of a military force unnecessary, for "behind the military men," wrote Villard, "and counting upon their aid and protection in overseas ventures, stand those who seek special privileges abroad or desire trading or manufacturing privileges at home." If armaments and the maintenance of a military force were rendered unnecessary, it would, according to Villard, "remove the heaviest financial burden from every nation, make possible the steady reduction of the hideous debts of the war and the carrying of the enormous pension payments which will result from the struggle, and should make impossible the excuse that we must tax imports in order to get money to carry on the government."

Third, tariffs cause waste and extravagance in business inasmuch as they help maintain numerous incompetent and unnecessary industries which would otherwise be forced out. They actually encourage inefficiency. What Americans needed to do to meet foreign competition, argued Villard, was "not to run away from it, but to improve our methods of production."

Fourth, the tariff, Villard feared, might open the way to socialization. In a letter to the editor of the British journal *Spectator*, Villard wrote that he had "never been able to see why Protection is not logically an entering wedge for the socialization of the industries involved." When the government voted a tariff schedule, ran Villard's argument, it went into partnership with each businessman for whose benefit it either checked or destroyed free competition from abroad and artificially limited the supply of goods available for use at home. In so doing, it robbed the protected industry of some of its "private" nature. Villard had no patience with the argument that the tariff helped maintain and protect a capitalistic system at home. If public aid was necessary, then private enterprise was no longer private and ought to be managed in the public interest:

> If it is right that the State should guarantee profits to anybody, why should it not guarantee those profits to itself? If there are certain industries deemed necessary to the well-being of the State which cannot be maintained without levying on the whole people for their support, it would surely produce a far better political atmosphere if the State were openly to carry them on instead of granting to certain favoured ones the licence to charge higher prices without any corresponding responsibility to or accounting to the State.

It should, perhaps, be reiterated here that Villard was not advocating socialism. He firmly and repeatedly repudiated the Socialist platform. His argument here is made against the tariff, which he did not think was necessary to the well-being of the economic system. He is arguing only that *if* such help were necessary, *then* it seemed to him socialism was justified.

Villard repeatedly attacked those tariff advocates who opposed government intervention in other areas. They were of the class of Herbert Hoover, who, posited Villard, did not see the "complete contradiction in his demand that the Government be kept out of private business and his insistence upon more and higher tariffs." The abolition of the tariff, as Villard saw it, meant a return to individual self-reliance and to business independence. Villard had other arguments against the tariff. Tariffs are a form of special privilege for which there is no place in a democracy. To seek out any one group for governmental favors, argued

Villard, "makes of the beneficiaries a specially favored class and favoritism of this kind is utterly repugnant to the spirit of true democracy or a sound Republic." Through the tariff the government fosters a caste system, made up of those "who for various reasons cannot make any money, or as much money as they would like to make. It is therefore," concluded Villard, "absolutely inimical to the doctrine of a square deal to all and no favors to any man." Tariffs become a means of extortion of the public by this privileged class. By using the tariff to assure themselves of high profits, the protected industries are able to extort higher and higher prices from the domestic consumer. The tariff is in effect a hidden tax, posited Villard. "It makes every citizen pay tribute to whoever has influence enough to get Congress to interfere with natural trade laws." So far as Villard could see, there had never been a tariff, Republican or Democratic, which did not shelter extortion and favoritism. And not until Hoover, he exhorted, had even the "wildest tariff maniac ever suggested that the tariff helped *everybody*." The recipients of tariff benefits were described by Villard as "hogs" who needed to be put in their "proper pens." The tariff was also politically corruptive: "You cannot put a political party in a position of dispensing tremendous tariff-favors, of regulating the size of the profits of any busines or industry," Villard wrote, "without inviting corruption. It is inevitable and inescapable." The tariff, as a privilege granted to a few, destroyed equality before the government and demoralized political parties generally. About its corrupting and demoralizing effects on political parties, Villard reported:

What results is that the Parties blackmail the manufacturers and the manufacturers blackmail the Parties. This is, of course, less true of the Democrats than the Republicans. For years the latter have "fried the fat" out of the manufacturers, as our political slang has had it, in order to fill their campaign coffers, and in return the manufacturers have demanded as their reward the fixing of tariff duties . . . More than one Presidential Election has been bought and sold in precisely this way.

What Villard termed the "buying and selling" of protective tariff favors had done more in his view to lower the standard of American politics than any other factor. Finally, the whole tariff system bore the stamp of immorality. It was immoral for the government to grant favors to any one group; it was immoral to tax the bulk of the people to support a privileged few; it was immoral for an elected representative to the United States Congress to support a tariff system which, according to Villard, "is steadily corrupting our political and economic life." He decried as immoral the logrolling tactics which Congressmen participated in over tariffs.

It might be noted in this connection that Villard held Congress, rather than the Executive, directly responsible for tariffs. He was little impressed, therefore, with the provisions of the Fordney-McCumber Act of 1922 which retained the Tariff Commission, originally established under President Wilson's administration in 1916, to facilitate a flexible tariff by recommending changes to the President, who could then proclaim new rates. Villard perceived that the Tariff Commission had come to be dominated by lobbyists and that its existence was in any case superfluous:

In the last analysis it is Congress that makes or unmakes tariffs, and not the President. Congress has permitted a

tariff commission to come into being only because it
knew that it would take forever to go through the whole
list of rates and that it could cut off the commission
whenever it saw fit. . . . to date the result of the commission's work has been a lowering of the tariff only on
Bob-White quail, Canadian-grown cherries, millfeed, cre-
sylic acid, and paintbrush handles.

Villard scoffed at the arguments put forth by tariff advocates. There was no menace from cheap foreign labor,
he claimed. It was the unit cost of an article, not the cost of
labor, which was the determining factor in price competition. That foreigners would benefit from our money
if Americans purchased from abroad was another fallacy.
It was not money per se that was important but the goods
and services which were purchased with it. Our high standard of living was not due to the tariff, posited Villard,
striking at another protectionist argument, but in spite of
it. Poor wages were paid in some of the most highly protected industries, as in textiles, for example. It was not
true either, said Villard, that foreigners really pay the
tax inherent in the tariff or that United States trade with
Japan was injurious. Actually, he argued, Japan had been
our best customer, and her trade had benefited thousands
of American workers.

The period around 1930 found Villard particularly in-
dignant over the sugar tariff as it affected the tiny republic
of Cuba. The Fordney-McCumber Act was up for revision
at this time, and Villard's hope was that the sugar tariff
would not be increased. Nationalism, extortion of our citizens, the benefits to businessmen of special privilege, and
the economic hardship imposed upon smaller nations—
all were inherent in the sugar tariff as it related to Cuba:

I should first of all abolish the sugar tariff against Cuba, an island almost within sight of our shores, whose sugar would come into our country free and untaxed if the American flag flew over Morro Castle in Havana; instead of which, merely because Cuba is outside of our national lines, we raise the price of sugar to every man, woman, and child and destroy the value of great American investments in that island. Also we help to reduce working masses in that country to misery and despair, and help to render them the helpless and hapless victims of a ruthless dictator—merely in order to insure profits to some of our citizens who unnecessarily entered the sugar business at home.

In a radio address entitled "Sugar and the Sugar Tariff," Villard gave vent to his disapproval of logrolling; he made light of the necessity of the tariff as a protection against infant industry—an argument he considered a smoke screen for the selfish interests of the protectionists—and portrayed close connection between business and politics. Villard waxed satirical:

Listen, tonight, for you shall hear the sweet saccharine story of sugar, and the sugar tariff, and how that tariff works so far as sugar is concerned, and why it is that we have a tariff at all . . . But this is just the way tariffs are made. Nothing scientific, nothing very honest about it, just a give and take log-rolling arrangement in Congress by which every fellow swaps his votes for protection for his beets or what not. It is politics and profits, with science and common sense nowhere, and much loud and baseless talk about necessary American infant industries, and its devil take the hindmost, and the hindmost, my dear friends, happen to be you who are listening to my voice, you plain, but innocent, and at present uninterested American consumers, who pay through the nose to support the sugar barons of Louisiana, and the beet sugar millionaires of Colorado.

Villard's efforts on behalf of Cuban sugar proved useless. The subsequent Smoot Amendment to the Smoot-Hawley Tariff Bill provided that the rate on Cuban sugar be increased from 1.76 cents per pound to 2 cents per pound.

Time after time throughout his administration, President Hoover defended the Smoot-Hawley Tariff Act. He defended it on the ground that it was the very basis of safety to agriculture, that there was no measure more vital to labor, and that during the depression it saved people from enormously increased unemployment. Villard was scornful. If tariffs were the blessing Herbert Hoover considered them to be, then, argued Villard, all forty-eight states ought to be surrounded with "those magic walls which are supposed to raise the standard of living and bestow prosperity upon all inside their circle." From Villard's point of view, the truth was quite to the contrary. Free trade was the only sound and rational policy for any country to adopt. The principle of free trade, he posited, was as sound as the principle that "men should be free and not enslaved, that people should determine their own fate and not foreigners who happen to be able to impose their will upon them by force." Not only was free trade sound, but Villard was convinced that it was workable. His stand was for a thoroughgoing elimination of the tariff system. In the presidential election of 1928, Villard considered tariff reform to be among the three big issues of the campaign; and

while he cast his vote for Alfred Smith, he took issue
with Smith over tariff reform. He rejected Smith's suggestion that the tariff be revised schedule by schedule. The only
solution Villard could or would envisage was "laying an axe
to the entire system." Two years later, he spoke in milder
tones but to practically the same effect. He proposed what
he termed a "gradual" approach in the direction of "tariffs
for revenue only" with the protection principle eliminated.

Later in the thirties, Villard was to support reciprocal
trade agreements as a step toward the complete and world-
wide free trade which he regarded as essential to peace,
prosperity, democracy, and honest government. But by
1947, in his last book, *Free Trade—Free World*, disillu-
sioned with the gradual approach, he was to scoff at these
agreements as compromises which served only to mitigate
protection.

The high tariffs of the twenties which Villard abhorred
can well be considered a form of subsidy, and as such he
sometimes referred to them. A more direct subsidy which
invited his indignation was government subsidization of
merchant shipping. During the war the government assumed the responsibility of providing the nation with a
merchant marine. In the early stages of formulating such
a policy, President Wilson had explored the matter with
Villard, whose reaction was that it "savoured of Socialism."
After the war pressure was exerted to turn merchant shipping back to private owners—a move of which Villard,
in his dedication to private initiative, approved. With the
advent of Republicans to power, the pressure became more
acute and finally resulted in the Merchant Marine Act of

1920 with its policy of quick and easy disposal of the merchant fleet to private operators. These operators, however, soon found themselves operating at a loss in competition with foreign lines. If the United States was to maintain the merchant fleet it required for the national defense, either government ownership or subsidy of private lines seemed necessary. Villard approved of neither course. He went so far as to acquire the *Nautical Gazette* to function as "an independent publication opposed to ship subsidies and a government-underwritten merchant marine." When the *Nautical Gazette* proved financially unrewarding, Villard turned to the pages of the *Nation* to advance his criticism of subsidies. He attacked ship subsidies on many of the same grounds on which he attacked tariffs. The government, through subsidies, was going into "partnership" with the operators; the subsidy was a form of "special privilege" in the sense that it guaranteed profits to certain businessmen without regard to their efficiency and competency; it was politically corruptive; ship subsidies were no more justified than subsidies to other necessities; they could be obviated by developing, on the part of our operators and builders, superior skill in construction and management. Villard added that such subsidies were a raid on the public treasury and a means of increasing the federal debt. Furthermore, a subsidized merchant reserve was no real security, dependent as it was on political fortunes. But another of Villard's causes was lost in the enactment of the Merchant Marine Act of 1928 which provided subsidized construction and operation costs and long-term mail-carrying contracts to private shippers.

Villard's rejection of what he considered government handouts in the years preceding the depression was thoroughgoing. It was not confined to subsidies to business but was applied to such areas as the veterans' bonus and farm benefits. As has already been noted, Villard was opposed to tariffs on agricultural commodities. The 1920's marked a decline in American agriculture. Land values and prices dropped, and the farmers were heavily in debt for their overexpansion during the war years. European markets were lost, and the farmers faced a growing surplus. The twenties gave rise to the controversial McNary-Haugen farm bills which called for price supports on farm goods, in addition to the agricultural tariffs already existent. Villard's *Nation* took a stand against the bills. "The farmers' salvation," declared the *Nation*, "lies chiefly in cooperation, in the abolition of the tariff, and in the opening up of foreign markets." On this particular issue, Villard's *Nation* joined President Coolidge as it had President Harding in support of laissez faire. Herbert Hoover assumed a like position: "No governmental agency should engage in buying and selling and price fixing of products." [7]

In June of 1929, however, Congress passed the Agricultural Marketing Act in response to Republican campaign promises of the previous fall for farm relief. This act rejected the price-fixing and subsidy features of the McNary-Haugen proposals. The Marketing Act created a Federal Farm Board which was to function, generally speaking, to encourage the organization and development of agricultural cooperatives, to make loans to those cooperatives, and to enter into agreements to insure the cooperatives against loss because of price declines. Up to this point, it was the

[7] William S. Myers (ed.), *The State Papers and Other Public Writings of Herbert Hoover* (New York: Doubleday & Co., Inc., 1934), I, 34.

kind of measure of which Villard approved. It was designed to help the farmers help themselves, without subsidy or the direct participation of government. The act, however, also provided that the Farm Board might create so-called "stabilization" corporations to purchase, handle, and market surpluses of particular commodities, thus repudiating Mr. Hoover's former stand. The Grain Stabilization and Cotton Stabilization corporations established thereby succeeded in pegging the market temporarily. They were caught, however, when they brought their operations to a terminal point, with surpluses which, in themselves, created problems and resulted in great cost to the public, to say nothing of the drastic fall in the prices of grains and cotton when the Farm Board withdrew. The Federal Farm Board lost $150,000,000 on cotton alone. Writing in 1930, before its full cost was known, Villard condemned this governmental venture into agriculture:

> I had expected that cries of socialism would be raised against it by an outraged business world, but business, suddenly acutely conscious of a falling-off in the farmers' buying power, did not make serious opposition. So the government supplied $200,000,000 to a board to coordinate the entire industry, to teach it to buy and sell cooperatively. But the Board went far beyond that, undertaking the suicidal policy of attempting from Washington to peg the prices of world commodities, with the result that its losses to date are variously estimated at between $40,000,000 and $50,000,000. Surely the government never went into business more deeply or more disastrously.

Two years later Villard was urging the gradual and voluntary creation of great cooperative farms, in an attempt to meet the problem of large industrial agricultural enterprises versus individual farming, a problem he deemed of major consequence. He hoped, too, that a way could be found to eliminate the middleman, so that the farmer "living within forty miles of our greatest cities would no longer get between three and five cents a quart for milk that sells at around fifteen on the streets."

The 1920's marked a new phase in the history of government relations with railroads. Prior to this period, railroad managers had opposed public control. Rapidly growing and powerful competition from pipe lines, motor vehicles, and waterways, however, sent railroad operators to Washington seeking protection; and governmental policy shifted from one of protecting the public against railroad abuses to one of keeping the roads operating in reasonable solvency. Villard's solution to the latter problem was government ownership and, if necessary, government operation. This may seem strange coming from the son of a railroad builder and president of four railroads and did in fact reflect a change in view point for Villard. As he explained in 1923:

I grew up in a school that believed wholeheartedly in private ownership and management of railroads. I have now reluctantly come to the conclusion that government ownership is absolutely essential to the welfare and economic development of the United States.

I hope that we shall be able to stave off government operation by joint management of the railroads on the part of the government, public, and workers, similar to that suggested by the Plumb Plan, but if no other way is open I am willing to accept government operation and ownership.

The railroads, as Villard saw them, were breaking down because of employee morale; they had become the creatures of special privilege. If the railroads, already subject to regulation, must now seek government financial aid, they ought to be taken over in the public interest.

By 1932 Villard was urging the amalgamation of the railroads into a national corporation to be managed by directors appointed by the government. This was the policy he was urging on the Governor of New York, at that time Franklin Delano Roosevelt, in anticipation of Roosevelt's candidacy for the Presidency. The kind of corporation Villard envisioned was similar to the Inland Waterways Corporation, an agency of the War Department which helped to develop navigation along the Ohio, Missouri, and Mississippi rivers with a resultant $6,000,000,000 a year business, offering stiff competition to rail carriers and making—in Villard's evaluation—"a complete success . . . where private capital facing private competition failed." Villard was more than ever concerned about the railroads at this time because of their failure to revive financially even after vast amounts of public funds had been poured into them through the Reconstruction Finance Corporation. Despite generous government loans, "one-third of the mileage was in bankruptcy. The roads were recognized as chronically sick, from reduced share of traffic, heavy debt, and duplication of services." [8]

Villard was further encouraged to support government ownership when Interstate Commerce Commissioner Joseph Eastman argued that government ownership, operation, and amalgamation were the best solution to the railroad dilemma. Villard, like Eastman and others, could see no future in maintaining individual railroad lines. It seemed highly practical and inevitable that the roads would become either a great private or a public system, for their financial survival rested in the great savings inherent in combinations and joint use of facilities. The thought of one great, *private* railroad trust was not, however, to Villard's liking. "Let our government return to a laissez faire policy for the railroads," he warned in defiance of trusts, "and a J. P. Morgan, a modern Harriman, or another James J. Hill would within the space of a very few years bring the railroads of the country under one control."

With railroad aid, as with tariffs, ship subsidies, and farm supports, Villard was fighting special privilege and needless expenditures of public funds for private interests. Whereas in the latter cases he opposed government participation, in the former he supported thoroughgoing government intervention. He maintained consistency by arguing in each case that socialization or nationalization was called for only when private enterprise absolutely could not do the job itself and the enterprise was essential to public welfare. The railroads, in Villard's mind, had reached that point. With regard to water power, natural resources, and utilities,

[8] Broadus Mitchell and Louise P. Mitchell, *American Economic History* (New York: Houghton Mifflin Co., 1947), p. 798.

Villard was to move an additional step toward more comprehensive governmental intervention in the economic sphere. In these areas he was motivated almost solely by a fear of the economic and political power inherent in their economic concentration.

During the 1920's there was increasing demand for federal supervision to check the growing economic strength of electric power companies and its concentration in a few hands through holding company management and control. With these demands came a movement toward public ownership and operation of power projects which had its inception in the Muscle Shoals project of the First World War. This movement was led in Congress by such liberals as Senators George Norris, Burton K. Wheeler, and Thomas I. Walsh. Throughout the twenties and into the thirties, Oswald Villard regularly and consistently spoke out for government retention and operation of Muscle Shoals, for a federal power installation on the Colorado River, and for public ownership and operation of the nation's water power in general. The La Follette platform which Villard supported in the 1924 presidential campaign included "public ownership of the nation's water power and the creation and development of a national super-water-power system, including Muscle Shoals." A similar plank was included in the 1925 platform of the Progressive Party of New York, with which Villard was closely associated. As with railroads, Villard feared the amalgamation of the nation's power companies into one great private concern. In 1930, speaking before the Virginia Institute of Public Affairs at Charlottesville, Villard explained that demand for a commission similar to the Interstate Commerce Commission to control private power companies was caused primarily by the belief that "if something is not done to check the combinations going on in this field there will soon be one company not only controlling all the power plants and public utilities in the United States but all those between the Rio Grande and the Straits of Magellen." [9] A month or so later, in a *Nation* article, Villard was more specific in his criticism: "If we retain the fee simple, we may grant licenses for operation under strict conditions insuring rates based on bona fide capital investment and not upon items such as huge and unreasonable fees to bankers, payment to lobbyists and other more than dubious items which have often been charged as part of the original investment."

Villard praised the water power policies of Alfred E. Smith and Franklin D. Roosevelt while each was Governor of New York State. Both favored state ownership and control of the state's power resources. Governor Smith made power policy the greatest single issue in his gubernatorial campaign of 1926 and made it clear that he sought to "retain and preserve the ownership of the source of supply for the people of the State." [10] In his 1928 Annual Message to the New York State Legislature, he reasserted his position:

There are but two roads upon which we can travel. There is no middle course. We must either take a chance and lease these properties for a term of years, which

[9] *New York Times,* Aug. 13, 1930, p. 18, col. 8.

[10] Alfred E. Smith, *Progressive Democracy: Addresses and State Papers of Alfred E. Smith* (New York: Harcourt, Brace & Co., 1928), p. 321.

really means giving them away with the possible right of recapture after we are all dead and gone . . . or declare for ourselves at once, retaining not only our full and complete ownership of these properties but the right to make contracts at rates favorable to the real owners of the power—the people of the State of New York.[11]

Of Alfred E. Smith, Villard once wrote approvingly that "he has fought all the great power combinations within the State, to prevent the exploitation by private capitalistic interests of what is the great heritage of all the people."

In 1932 Villard urged Franklin D. Roosevelt to apply the same principles to the power problem which he had enunciated as Governor of New York State and to favor government operation and distribution of power at Boulder Dam and Muscle Shoals. Roosevelt, too, had taken the position that New York State power belonged to the people but, like Smith before him, was unable to secure his objective because of Republican opposition in both Albany and Washington.

Villard was just as insistent that government take over other natural resources. Oil, timber, coal, and iron were among the resources he sought to protect. The Teapot Dome scandal of the Harding administration which involved the secret leasing of naval oil reserves to powerful operators Harry F. Sinclair and Edward L. Doheny, not only to their own financial benefit but to that of Secretary of the Interior Albert B. Fall as well, had shocked Villard. Indictments for conspiracy and bribery were brought against Fall, Doheny, and Sinclair in June, 1924—the month in which the Republican National Convention met to nom-

[11] *Ibid.*, p. 333.

inate its presidential candidate for the forthcoming election. Villard satirically referred to the convention as that of the "fit-to-rule." He was embittered by the fact that, in the face of the Teapot Dome scandal, the convention had the hypocrisy to go on record, in the name of the "Great Conservationist," Theodore Roosevelt, in favor of protection of natural resources: "All of its specious promises that the conservation policies of Theodore Roosevelt should be maintained and the oil and timber and unoccupied coal lands should be reserved for the people, the delegates swallowed with their tongues in their cheeks—all that the Sinclairs and Dohenys and the timber and coal barons have not yet got." The "Progressive" platform which Villard supported in that same presidential election year called for strict public control and permanent conservation of all the nation's resources, including coal, iron and other ores, oil, and timber lands. In the following year, 1925, the platform of the Progressive Party of New York, to most of which Villard subscribed, supported "public ownership and operation of the nation's natural resources such as coal, iron, oil, timber." By 1927 Villard was expressing discouragement at the progress made in protecting natural resources. "Who speaks now of the popular control of our natural resources?" he queried; and among the twelve points he offered as a basis on which to take up the reform movement of the early 1900's, which had been abandoned because of the war, was government ownership of natural resources, of water power, and of mines.

The years 1930 and 1931 saw extensive unrest and agitation in the mining industries. Organized miners were forced to take a reduction in wages, and there was widespread unemployment because of competition from the nonunion fields in some of the southern states, among which was West Virginia. Speaking before the West Virginia Editorial Association on October 30, 1931, Villard once more took the now-familiar position that if an industry could not survive under private enterprise then the government should take it over. And he applied this theory to iron as well as to coal, in spite of the fact that he was the owner and operator of the Fort Montgomery Iron Company:

> I am a mine owner, and a mine operator myself, and also, as it happens, on the verge of bankruptcy. . . . but I say to you that if the conditions in your distressed mining fields cannot be remedied by the operators, or by such powers of protest as the working man may have, or by both working together then I think that they should be put out of business, and the mines taken over by the government.

Among those measures of the Hoover administration for which Villard had respect was the President's withdrawal of all oil lands from leasing except those leases which had been made mandatory by Congress. Villard ultimately wanted government ownership and operation not only of oil wells but of pipe lines as well. He also favored socialization of radio, telephone, telegraph, and general utilities. Of the latter, Villard said (facetious only in the assumption of the dictator role), "If I were dictator . . . I should enormously lighten the burden of taxation by having the profits of public utilities go into the pockets not of stockholders, but of the communities which operate them, or into a general treasury."

A fair statement of Villard's position on natural resources

and utilities is found in the four-year presidential plan prepared by the League for Independent Political Action in 1932. This was a plan which the league felt any President with social vision and a progressive political party behind him could initiate and in part achieve between the years 1932 and 1936. The plan, point by point, was almost identical with Villard's own position, and he hopefully published it in its entirety in the *Nation* of February 17, 1932. With regard to power and public utilities the league took the position that

> Private ownership of the power industry and public utilities has resulted in evils intolerable in a democracy. Regulation has failed to protect the public interest and has proved a source of corruption of government because profits of power monopolies and other utility companies are so great as to form irresistible incentive for breaking down and controlling regulation and undermining the integrity of government. Public utility companies have established the greatest racket in the world, taking each year from the pockets of American workers at least $500,000,000 through unfair charges and excess rates. Experience has shown that regulation cannot be relied upon to protect the public.

The plan endorsed immediate federal ownership and operation of Muscle Shoals and other federal power projects; federal and state legislation to carry out the project of public ownership and operation of power and public utilities; and legislation providing for control of coal, oil, and railroads in the public interest, looking forward to eventual public ownership.

A characteristic feature of the economic system of the twenties was consolidation. In all industries there was a trend toward merger and amalgamation. A common strand may be seen running through Villard's considerations of the railroad problem and of private versus public power, namely his fear of consolidation, of trusts, and of monopoly. This fear was also part of his insistence on government ownership of natural resources. "More and more people are beginning to see," he wrote, "that uncontrolled exploitation of natural resources means . . . ruin of the small producers." Yet Villard saw the apparent inevitability of big business in a complex, industrialized society. As close as he was to La Follette's 1924 presidential campaign, he criticized La Follette's position on the trust question as "backward," for it called for the use of federal power only "to crush private monopoly, not to foster it." To Villard's mind, La Follette's position in practice meant the enforcement of the Sherman Act and the criminal prosecution of those who indulged in monopoly or trade agreements. Villard argued that such a measure was unrealistic: "Our economic and industrial situation has gone far beyond the imprisonment of a few trust heads and the dissolution of a few more trusts so that their individual parts may wax greater than ever by arriving at the same result in other ways. We cannot return to the era of small business if we would." As long as big business was here to stay, Villard was convinced that government ownership in some fields and the threat of it in others were the only methods which would bring an end to the waste, duplication, and other evils of large-scale industry. He did not share Herbert Hoover's faith that business could successfully police itself.

When Hoover became Secretary of Commerce in 1921, he was convinced that industrial waste, unfair practices, and other abuses could be eliminated without destruction of either equality of opportunity or individual initiative through cooperative action on the part of industry. He recommended, consequently, that the Sherman Act be amended to allow the establishment of trade associations. These associations were to perform a number of functions. Among them were the preparation of statistical abstracts from information supplied by the members as a guide to future production; the standardization of products along the lines of variety, grade, and quality; adoption of uniform credit policies; settlement of trade disputes by arbitration instead of litigation; elimination of unfair practices and misrepresentation of goods; promotion of uniform improvement of working conditions; cooperation for economy in insurance; establishment of common agencies to handle all problems of transportation; and cooperative research.

Following Hoover's suggestions, American industry between 1921 and 1925 became a vast superstructure of trade and industrial associations. Villard looked upon them with skepticism and disfavor:

> In view of the fact President Hoover is reported to be in favor of repealing the Sherman Anti-Trust Act, and has encouraged the coming together of manufacturers in all lines of enterprise to formulate intertrade agreements in order to cut out waste, duplication, and the creation of unnecessary articles, the question is sometimes raised whether we are not coming to the Communist ideal from another point of approach. . . . Certainly fewer and

fewer people believe that the private-profit motive when left alone to exploit the riches of the earth is harmless, or even beneficial in the absence of monopoly.

Thus Villard puts an ironic twist to the proposal of rugged individualist Herbert Hoover.

The 1920's comprised a period of high prosperity for most Americans, the farmer being a major exception. There was widespread enjoyment of a high level of wages, tremendous capitalist expansion, and a heavy production and consumption of new goods. Between 1930 and 1932, however, production decreased 36 per cent; labor income decreased 40 per cent; and the farmer's income decreased 50 per cent. In April of 1930 there were approximately 3,187,000 unemployed. By February of 1932 the figures are calculated to have reached 10,000,000 unemployed, while at the lowest point of the depression—1933—there were probably 15,000,-000 unemployed. Poverty, starvation, and a housing shortage accompanied the prostration of business.

The Hoover administration proceeded in the face of the depression to argue that the economic structure of the country was basically sound and that the solution to the economic ills of the United States rested on voluntary cooperation of business, labor, and agriculture, along with reliance on individual initiative. Hoover attempted to get industry voluntarily to adopt construction programs, to maintain wages, and to check the discharge of employees. He asked labor to cooperate by refraining from striking for wage increases. The government itself undertook an expanded federal building program, and Hoover urged states and municipalities to do likewise. The Federal Farm Board was established to help agriculture secure higher prices, and the Reconstruction Finance Corporation was established to make government credits available to banks, credit companies, insurance companies, and railroads.

To alleviate unemployment, which with its accompanying hardships was the most serious problem confronting the nation in 1931 and 1932, Hoover's administration took such steps as curtailing immigration and establishing a Committee for Unemployment Relief to coordinate the relief program of private, state, and local agencies. When the demand was made for direct federal aid to the unemployed, however, Hoover refused:

> This is not an issue as to whether people should go hungry or cold in the United States. It is solely a question of the best method by which hunger and cold shall be prevented. It is a question as to whether the American people on one hand will maintain the spirit of charity and mutual self help through voluntary giving and the responsibility of local government as distinguished on the other hand from appropriations out of the Federal Treasury for such purposes. My own conviction is strongly that if we break down this sense of responsibility of individual generosity to individual and mutual self help in the country in times of national difficulty and if we start appropriations of this character we have not only impaired something infinitely valuable in the life of the American people but have struck at the roots of self-government.[12]

[12] Myers, *op. cit.*, p. 496.

Unfortunately for Mr. Hoover's philosophy, the funds of private charitable organizations were soon exhausted, and additional donations were not forthcoming in the face of the severe and uncertain economic situation facing most Americans. As for state and local governments, the relief burden was too much for them. Oswald Garrison Villard was sharp, cynical, and bitter in his condemnation of Mr. Hoover's refusal to sanction relief legislation:

> Nowhere will it appear on the statute books that, during the greatest economic crisis which has ever confronted the United States, so far not one single dollar has been spent as an opiate of Government charity. Americans may be dying of starvation . . . but if that is the case they are dying with their systems undrugged and their characters unbesmirched by anything approaching a dole—a dole to Mr. Hoover is apparently the final act of perfidy of any government.

Yet Hoover's administration through the Reconstruction Finance Corporation alone channeled millions of dollars into an attempt to strengthen banks, railroads, and corporations and passed the Smoot-Hawley Tariff, the highest in United States history. With reference to the men who profited by what Villard considered governmental favors, he commented caustically:

> They, like President Hoover, believe that a government's giving cash to a needy individual destroys that man's moral fiber, weakens his character, and robs him of initiative, self-reliance, and self-respect. Yet they are quite certain that governmental grants to what they consider needy

corporations have none of these evil effects upon the character, or practices, or initiative, or self-reliance of the
several corporate managements.

Hoover seemed convinced that the measures his administration was taking were not only correct but corrective.
His administration issued periodic optimistic statements
about the immediacy of recovery. Characteristic is a statement of the President himself on May 1, 1930. "I am convinced," he told the United States Chamber of Commerce,
"we have now passed the worst and with continued unity of
effort we shall rapidly recover. There is one certainty in the
future of a people of the resources, intelligence, and character of the people of the United States—that is, prosperity." [13] Villard received Hoover's optimism with humor-
ous contempt. "For Mr. Hoover and his Cabinet, and other
talkers of economic nonsense," he wrote, "I should reserve
the Island of Yap with the requirement that morning and
evening they should meet together to inform one another
that prosperity is just around the corner, and that every day
in every way things are getting better and better."

By 1931 Villard was greatly distressed at the poverty in
the midst of plenty which was reflected in the fact that many
Americans were quite literally starving while the government held, through the Federal Farm Board, huge surpluses
of grain. It was not until the spring of 1932 that some of
the Farm Board's holdings were turned over to the Red
Cross for channeling to the nation's needy.

Demands for more direct and extensive intervention by
government to relieve conditions and bolster the economy
became insistent. The usual proposals for government action

[13] *Ibid.*, p. 289.

included government control over capital allocations for
productive purposes only, price control, a public works
program, an increase in labor's purchasing power, and government ownership in those areas where natural monopoly
prevailed—the railroads and public utilities for example.
Villard endorsed these proposals and added others. His personal program to meet the emergency included radical reduction or abolition of tariffs; cancellation or drastic reduction of reparations and war debts (There was no hope for
American recovery, posited Villard, until Europe was well
along the way to economic rehabilitation.); government
ownership and operation of railroads; reduction of government waste in veterans' services and military and naval expenditures; introduction of the five-day week and removal
of children under eighteen years of age from all industry;
mandatory nation-wide adoption of an old-age pension
similar to that of New York State; a comprehensive unemployment insurance program; and national support of the
unemployed wherever it was impossible for cities and states
to carry the load. Villard offered two approaches to the last
proposal: first, the adoption of large-scale public works
programs to be financed by a bond flotation and devoted
particularly to the rebuilding of cities to eliminate slums; and
second, direct monetary payments to the unemployed. "We
spend billions to kill Germans," complained Villard, refer-
ring to the war, "why not spend billions to keep Americans
alive?" Villard's plan for the financing of such a proposal
was the flotation of a long-term loan of $2,000,000,000. Sim-
ilar to wartime bonds, these were to bear a reasonable rate of
interest and be issued in small denominations. Villard was
confident that the loan would be subscribed because those
who were hoarding their savings would find in the bonds
the absolutely safe investment they were searching for. Of

the $2,000,000,000 to be raised in this fashion, Villard pro-
posed the use of $1,200,000 to be disbursed through states
and localities to the unemployed; $400,000,000 to be spent on
converting empty buildings and erecting barracks for home-
less unemployed who were willing to labor on public works
programs for room and board; and $400,000,000 to be used
in an attempt to keep the farmer on the farm.

Villard argued that his measures were designed not only
to meet the immediate problems of the time but to provide
a general overhauling of the economic system in the firm
conviction that it was underdistribution rather than over-
production which was the main problem facing the American economy. According to Villard, recovery depended
upon the restoration of purchasing power to the masses, a
view which was shared by neither businessmen nor the busi-
ness-dominated administration. Business interests refused to
admit that there was anything fundamentally wrong with
the economic system of the United States. To Villard they
were extremely shortsighted, if not totally blind, in not being able to see a causal relationship between existing social
institutions and the severe depression with which the country was faced: "If we work out of this situation they will
wish to go on doing business just as before, supremely
happy in their belief that they alone are fit to rule us, without making the slightest effort to reorganize our social, political, or economic life." Villard was insistent on the point that
our economic and political systems were faulty and that recovery could not be achieved without reform. His observa-
tion of conditions and events in other parts of the world
served only to re-enforce his convictions:

If we are to do anything else but drift we must recognize
the fact that the competitive system has failed at many

points, must begin to do at once what has been done abroad—formulate far-reaching economic and political programs to deal with the new situation. Sooner or later this will have to be done. We too are part of a world current; it is sweeping us onward. Shall we drift through the rapids without thought as to what may happen to us, or shall we set ourselves a course and hold it true? That is the question which confronts us all.

The turning point for the United States was to take place with the Democratic victory of 1932. The discrediting of the business leadership of the twenties paved the way for concerted governmental intervention in economic affairs and for far-reaching reforms. The action for which Villard and other liberals had pleaded for more than a decade was forthcoming with Franklin D. Roosevelt's assumption of the Presidency and his pursuance of a New Deal for the American people which spelled an end to laissez faire.

American liberals came to discard laissez faire, in its implication of rugged individualism, as an outmoded, unworkable doctrine. In its search for social justice, American liberalism committed itself to the use of governmental power and agencies to remedy those evils, environmental and economic, from which the less fortunate classes suffered. American liberalism became concerned with the welfare of ordinary men and particularly those who were at the greatest economic disadvantage under a newly emerged economic structure. Liberalism was to attempt in the 1930's to maintain or re-create in the individual a sense of self-respect even in the face of economic insecurity. It was to seek higher standards in a host of aspects of social life.

CHAPTER VIII

Approach to Internationalism and Pacifism

INTERNATIONALISM AND PACIFISM as aspects of American liberalism have embraced an understanding of foreign nations, a respect for their people, a sympathy for their problems, and a desire to work cooperatively with them on matters of mutual interest in order that peace and harmony among nations may prevail.

Such an attitude is consistent, for the most part, with the philosophic tenets of American liberalism. Indeed, it is an attempt to apply those tenets in the international sphere. Humanism and individualism, for example, are concerned for the happiness, freedom, and progress of *all* mankind and assume the dignity and worth of every human being. Humanitarianism is an extension of the Christian doctrine that *all* men *everywhere* are created equal in the sight of God and by the law of the universe. Rationalism assumes that the problems of organized society can be solved by men through reason and without recourse to violence. The acceptance of internationalism by the American liberal seems only logical if viewed as an attempt on the part of the liberal to guarantee in the international sphere the same degree of morality, of political and economic freedom, and of respect for the individual as he sought to establish at home.

The liberalism of pacifism is rooted in rationalism as well as humanitarianism. The former allows for the assumption that nations, like individuals, can find rational modes of conducting their relations with one another and reasonable solutions to their problems. It is not, therefore, surprising to find that Oswald Garrison Villard assumed a strong internationalist and pacifist position throughout the 1920's. His was a keen and lively interest in almost every issue which arose in the international sphere during that period, combined with a violent hatred of war. He spoke out vigorously and effectively against war and on behalf of the search for peaceful means of settling international problems; he advocated self-government for all nations throughout the world; he attacked American imperialism wherever it was evidenced.

Villard's views on international affairs reflected always a respect for and generosity toward alien peoples—an attitude he attributed at least in part to the influence of Henry Villard, his father. Villard once wrote of his father, "Citizen of two lands, no narrow nationalism could be his. He abhorred those who seek by metes and bounds to stake out for their selfish selves a part of the world to have it all their own, letting the devil take care of the rest. He felt the world should be as free as the air . . . He hated no man for his color, and feared none because his was a different hue, a different tongue, another faith, a strange and baffling mode of life." Henry Villard's influence on his son's attitudes was felt on yet another matter. Oswald Villard wrote of him, "He, long a leader in large affairs, friend of all the statesmen of his time, who had given his life to practical constructive effort, revolted with his whole soul from that sum of all villainies, war, which turns men into beasts, which destroys and never builds up, and never leaves the world but worse. Is it any wonder that he who writes this should share these views?" [1] Oswald Garrison Villard's categorical opposition to war as a mode of solving disputes among nations was sustained throughout the whole of his adult life.

As early as April 24, 1915, Oswald Garrison Villard addressed a meeting of the Massachusetts Branch of the Women's Peace Party. He took the occasion to urge a new seat in the Cabinet of the President of the United States, namely that of Secretary of Peace, whose objective would be to divert to the cause of the maintenance of peace a portion of the $147,000,000 of federal funds allocated to the Navy. Said Villard, "The militarists have done badly since 1900. Give the Pacifists a chance. Let us try our hand. God knows we can't do any worse." [2]

Villard did not intend facetiousness in making this suggestion. From the Spanish-American War on, he was a dedicated pacifist. He belonged to a number of voluntary organizations dedicated to the cause of peace. Among them were the American Union Against Militarism, the Church Peace Union, the Committee on Militarism in Education, the Keep America Out of War Congress, the National Peace Conference, the New York Peace Society, and the Women's International League for Peace and Freedom. Indeed, it was Villard's uncompromising pacifism which led indirectly

[1] See "A True Fairy Tale," in Sydney Strong (ed.), *What I Owe to My Father* (New York: Henry Holt & Co., Inc., 1931), pp. 157–58.

[2] *New York Times*, April 25, 1915, sec. III, p. 3, col. 4.

to his relinquishment of the *Evening Post* during the First World War and directly to his final break with the editorial staff of the *Nation* just prior to the United States's entrance into the Second World War.

Villard's hatred of war was based on moral, practical, and philosophical grounds. The moral problem posed by war was violation of the Christian ethic in that it was "faithless to our belief in Jesus and to our belief in everything God-like in man," and again Villard put conscience above obedience to the state. Deploring the growing militarism of the United States, Villard wrote, "There are many things above the State and superior to it, and one of these is Christianity. Where the teachings of Jesus and allegiance to the State conflict, you will invariably find me putting Jesus above the State. Reverence for the State? . . . Why *should* we reverence it? It is meant to be the servant of peoples, and it has become their master and beyond their control, slaughtering millions as it will."

On the practical side, the effects of war were uncontrollable. "If you go to war," argued Villard, "you cannot tell where the war will end any more than you can prophesy the date of its conclusion. Its ramifications are endless; its reverberations carry to the ends of the earth." Villard, for example, attributed to the war the scandals of the Harding administration. The war, Villard argued, put an end to Wilson's New Freedom; and the debate over the League of Nations and Wilson's subsequent unpopularity led to the victory of the Republicans in 1920 with its return to conservatism and materialism as reflected in the Teapot Dome scandal: "The crassest of materialism reigns in Washington by grace of Woodrow Wilson's plunge into war, and where materialism is there sits corruption. The Denbys, the Falls, the Daughertys, the Dohenys, now all condemned by one court or another, are some of the responses to the appeals for war, to the setting free of the passions that war spells. These are some of the most striking results of the effort to achieve righteousness at home and abroad by unparalleled blood-letting." Pragmatically Villard could never conceive of war as a means to the solution of a problem or the attainment of an objective, no matter how difficult the problem or how admirable the aim. Villard once quoted Franklin K. Lane, Secretary of the Interior under President Woodrow Wilson, as saying that "life is just a beautiful adventure, to be flung away for any good cause," and Villard was quick to point out that not only was the "manner of the flinging" important, but one had to be quite certain of the cause: "He [Lane] lived to see a hundred thousand young Americans make a beautiful adventure of their precious young existences, at the behest of Mr. Wilson and his Cabinet, flinging them away for some exquisitely painted ideals which have not materialized and will not materialize in any such way."

Villard's position on the futility of war was stated explicitly and eloquently in the *Nation:*

You may glorify the struggle as you will, and supply it, if you please, with aims as lofty as you can possibly portray by pen or voice; you may attribute to yourself and your allies the purest motives, the noblest objectives, the most humanitarian desires. You will inevitably fail to achieve those ends, and your beautifully cadenced words will turn to ashes because it is ordained by the way of the world that goodness and virtue, the safeguarding of human rights and what is called civilization can never be achieved by letting loose hell upon earth.

Villard's case in point was, of course, the First World War. Not only did it fail to achieve the aims set forth by President Wilson, particularly the furtherance of democracy and the guarantee of the rights of small nations, but its aftermath was, in Villard's view, a situation even worse than that which had existed prior to it. Writing in 1927, he said:

Each passing year has made plainer that democracy was never so unsafe, that the rights of small nations were never so jeopardized—those small nations to whom Mr. Wilson pledged the victory, and "the privilege of men everywhere to choose their way of life and obedience." His own nation still subjugates Haiti . . . it still overruns Nicaragua with marines, and threatens Mexico because its people demand the "privilege of men everywhere to choose their way of life and of obedience." To Russians we deny this same privilege because we hate the form their revolution has taken, and think infinitely more of our individual properties than of their human rights.

. . . . .

In eleven European countries despots wipe their feet upon the prostrate bodies of Liberty and Democracy.

On the philosophic side, war violated the liberal tenets of humanitarianism, rationalism, and individualism. Villard saw in war the negation of liberalism. He once commented, again with reference to Franklin K. Lane, that "great liberal that Mr. Lane was, he had not learned the lesson that when war touches liberalism it shrivels and withers where it does not utterly destroy it." On another occasion, Villard wrote that "only one thing is certain: Wherever war, there liberty shrivels, lies insensate—dies."

It should be noted that pacifist liberals have not always embraced the absolute pacifist position, that is, opposition to any participation in war under all circumstances. The pacifist liberal has not always been nonresistant and has, for example, lent his support to a defense against invasion or, once the nation was at war, supported the war effort. Indeed, even the peace societies subordinated their principles to the pursuit of Allied victory once the United States had entered the war.

Much as he abhorred war, Villard's pacifist position, too, was not of the extreme right. Once the United States had entered World War I, Villard, like others, was concerned that the victory should be an Allied one: "We were in the war and those of my faith certainly did not want the Germans to win and hoped from our hearts that, if the war must be fought to a finish on the battlefields, our troops would speedily end it. The last thought of any of us would have been to put obstacles in the way." [3] Although Villard refused to lend his approval to the war and would have refused to bear arms if called upon, he nevertheless performed those services which were within the bounds of his conscience. He recalls those activities in *Fighting Years:*

> I had hoped from the beginning to enter some non-military governmental service. Here, as at other points, the dissenters were divided as to how far they could go. It was obvious that one could not escape participating in the war, try as one might, for every railroad, theatre and

[3] Villard, *Fighting Years*, pp. 326–27.

concert ticket, every stamp purchased and all taxes paid contributed to the war. I, for one, freely bought Liberty bonds and conformed otherwise where I conscientiously could. As president of the Dobbs Ferry Hospital, for whose initial construction I and one other had raised the funds, plus a bequest from my father, I took the lead in offering its services to the government and so, far from being indifferent to the needs of wounded soldiers, contributed freely to relief agencies, specifying, however, in the case of the Red Cross, that my gift should be earmarked to be used only for reconstruction in France.[4]

Whether or not Villard could ever have brought himself to approve of United States participation in war is difficult to judge. He held consistently, from as early as 1917 on, to the position that the commitment of the United States to war was a policy which only the voters should decide, and Villard gave the impression that he would be willing to abide by the results of a referendum. "But should the people at large decide for war," he once commented, "it is a long-time American habit for all to bow to the will of the whole people." [5] One tends to suspect, however, that had a referendum decided in favor of war, Villard not only would have considered the majority in error but would have resorted to the argument that even a majority vote could not make war morally right. Villard, however, was convinced in his own mind that the majority of the people of the United States did not favor participation in World War I but that their views were not heard above the clamor of the few who favored participation and who controlled the bulk of the American

[4] *Ibid.*, pp. 332–33.
[5] *New York Times*, Feb. 19, 1917, p. 2, col. 6.

press: "Many hundreds of thousands who were opposed to our going to war, and are opposed to it now, still feel that their views—as opposed to those of the prosperous and intellectual classes—were not voiced in the press last winter. They know that their position today is being misrepresented as disloyal or pro-German by the bulk of the newspapers."

In the debate in the Senate which followed President Wilson's request for a declaration of war, liberal Senators Vardaman, Norris, and La Follette expressed these same views. Senator James K. Vardaman (Democrat, Mississippi), for example, declared that, even to liberate Germany from the cruel domination of kings, he could not vote for sacrificing a million men without first consulting the people to be sacrificed for that deliverance.[6] Norris of Nebraska bitterly accused munitions makers, stockbrokers, bond dealers, and a servile press of being responsible for the catastrophe at hand: "We are going into war upon the command of gold . . . I feel that we are committing a sin against humanity and against our countrymen." [7] La Follette, too, called attention to the lack of a medium through which the people could voice their opinion: "The President of the United States, in his message of the 2nd of April, said that the European war was brought on by Germany's rulers without the sanction or will of the people. For God's sake, what are we doing now? Does the President of the United States feel that the will of the American people is being consulted in regard to this declaration of war? The people of Germany surely had as much consideration as he has given the people of the United States." [8]

[6] *Congressional Record*, 65th Cong., 1st sess., April 4, 1917, pp. 208–11.

[7] *Ibid.*, p. 214.   [8] *Ibid.*, April 5, 1917, p. 372.

In Villard's eyes, the war-making power in the United States which constitutionally belongs to Congress had been shifted to the Executive:

Under the constitution, the power to make war is vested in the Congress, but this clause is as much a dead letter today as the 14th and 15th Amendments . . . . The war-making power has been taken over by the President of the United States, partly against the wish of the Congress, partly because of its indifference or by its consent . . . the Executive has developed a technique, as Mr. Wilson proved at the time of our going into the World War, which makes it possible for him to reduce Congress to absolute submission. Given a period of public hysteria, of a press stirred to sensationalism by the possibility of a conflict, and a President determined upon having his way, and Congress is practically helpless. The President may march an army into foreign territory, or send a fleet to bombard a helpless foreign city, as Mr. Wilson did in 1915, and the country is committed before Congress can act. Then it is only necessary to call upon the country to stand by the President and the flag, and the thing is done.

However, Villard argued that the real issue was not the respective rights of Congress and the President in making war but was rather a question of whether either one of them should have that power:

What the situation not only of this country, but of the entire world calls for is the limitation of the war-making power of both Congress and the Executive. Wars, as we all know, have now entirely changed their character . . . Conscription and the great development of the art of war, has so changed things that when hostilities begin the entire population is at once affected. . . . the victims suffer economically just as much as the vanquished . . . The question, therefore, arises whether this dreadful power of making war should hereafter be intrusted to any Executive, any Cabinet, and any Congress.

As might well be expected, Villard answered in the negative. "My answer," he said, "is no; that the delegation of this power by the people to their chosen representatives must be revoked; that only the people themselves, who pay the price of modern war, shall have the right to decide whether a cause for war exists, and whether the nation shall make the sacrifices which such a struggle involves."

Villard's ultimate objective, however, was not the guarantee that war would be waged only with popular consent but rather that war would not be waged at all. He reasoned that the mutual distaste for war of people everywhere would render their consent impossible to attain. He reasoned further that once the fear of war and sudden attack had been dispelled from the atmosphere in which international relations were conducted war itself might be precluded.

One of the roots of liberalism is opposition to compulsion or coercion. This, indeed, is the meaning of liberty. Insistence upon freedom or noncoercion makes a liberal oppose war and makes it difficult for him to sanction the maintenance of a large military establishment designed as an instrument of coercion. Indeed, Villard was convinced that a chief cause of World War I was Prussian militarism, and it was a fear of encouraging the military spirit that was the basis of his opposition to universal military training and the assembling of armaments in peacetime. Thus, throughout the debate over preparedness in the three years immediately preceding World War I, Villard joined such liberals as Lillian Wald, John Dewey, Jane Addams, and President Alexander Meiklejohn of Amherst College in opposing military training. Villard refuted the arguments put forth by advocates of military training to the effect that military service would "discipline our lawless youth, act as a tonic to democracy, promote industrial efficiency and 'furnish America with a soul.' " [9] The *New York Times* reports Villard as maintaining that the "stuff and balderdash" of some prominent men that war was necessary "to keep up the manly virtues" of a race had been exposed by the fighting qualities shown by nations which had long been at peace.[10] Ideas such as these undoubtedly suggested to Villard the Prussianism of men like Friedrich von Bernhardi and Heinrich von Treitschke. Always Villard's opposition to military training reflected a fear of stimulating enthusiasm for militarism in these United States—a spirit which Villard felt could lead only to war.

Toward the end of 1916, the American Union Against Militarism, of which Villard was a member of the executive committee, made a desperate last attempt to forestall compulsory universal military training by bringing pressure to bear on the Congressional Military Affairs Committee. The union took the position that if an armed force had to be raised, then it should be raised by voluntary enlistment. Villard maintained that compulsory universal military training

[9] Quoted in Merle Curti, *Peace or War: The American Struggle, 1636–1936* (New York: W. W. Norton & Co., Inc., 1936), p. 235.

[10] *New York Times*, March 28, 1915, sec. II, p. 18, col. 1.

was a good imitation of the Prussian method of government. He reiterated his distaste for such methods when he insisted, "I do not believe in combating this abominable Prussianism the world is facing by Prussian methods of warfare or by killing to put an end to war." [11] At another time Villard, in criticizing the Army General Staff, charged that it had "out-Prussianized Germany" in its demand for a standing army of 286,000 men. Villard also argued that it was "not in accordance with the principles of American Government to pursue such a large military scheme." [12]

When it became clear that compulsory military service was inevitable, pacifist groups attempted to obtain complete exemption from conscription for those men conscientiously opposed to war. Villard likened the desired exemption to exemption from jury duty in a murder trial: "The difference between compulsory jury duty and compulsory taxes which are sometimes compared to compulsory military service, is that the moral law, 'Thou Shalt Not Kill' is at stake. All men are today excused from jury duty in a murder case who are opposed to putting a human being to death. A similar privilege is all we pacifists shall ask if this nation decides for compulsory training." [13] Villard undertook to persuade the government to adopt a reasonable policy for conscientious objectors. With the assistance of Roger Baldwin, he prepared a plan which embraced the concept of farm camps where the conscientious objectors would raise food for the Army. President Wilson seemed sympathetic. He wrote his secretary, Joseph Tumulty, to "Please thank Mr. Villard of *The Evening Post* for his memorandum which you sent me

[11] *Ibid.*, Feb. 13, 1917, p. 9, col. 2.
[12] *Ibid.*, March 18, 1917, p. 5, col. 6.
[13] *Ibid.*, Feb. 13, 1917, p. 9, col. 3.

about the conscientious objectors. It contains a great deal that is interesting and sensible, and I am sure that it will be read with as much sympathetic appreciation by the Secretary of War, to whom I am sending it, as by myself." [14]

The policy toward the objectors which was adopted, however, did not embody Villard's plan. This policy required exempts to perform a substitute noncombatant service within the military establishment or serve a jail term. There were fewer than 4,000 conscientious objectors in the First World War, and all but 450 accepted an alternate form of service. Of these 450, Villard's friend Roger Baldwin was one who spent some months in prison. Villard wrote Baldwin in the Essex County, New York, jail in praise of his pacifist stand: "Seriously, you did a wonderful service and I am more proud than I can say to have known you." Villard was contemptuous of the jail sentence as a means of reprisal against conscientious objectors. Stupid governments everywhere, he wrote in verse, would never learn that:

> High walls and huge the BODY may confine,
>   And iron grates obstruct the prisoner's gaze,
> And massive bolts may baffle his design,
>   And vigilant keepers watch his devious ways:
> Yet scorns the immortal MIND this base control!
>   No chains can bind it, and no cell enclose:
> Swifter than light, it flies from pole to pole,
>   And, in a flash, from earth to heaven it goes!

Villard began, before the war was over, to urge the disarmament of all nations—a disarmament which was to include the abolition of universal conscription. He proposed

[14] Quoted in Villard, *Fighting Years*, pp. 334–35.

that each nation be enabled to maintain only "small armed constabularies, but permit of the maintenance of no troops trained for war . . . Militarism grows upon the exercise of the military habit," he continued, "and no nation, in my judgment, can escape it which goes in for a large military or naval class." On another occasion Villard indicated the size of the force he thought the United States should maintain: "Now I want to see the United States of its own accord, return to its military and naval status of 1898 when our Army comprised only 25,000 men and the militia 100,000." Villard reiterated his fear of the military mind: "To me, the greatest menace in the world is the military and naval mind, and it is the same everywhere. Hence our first objective should be the mustering out of these minds." In part serious and partly in jest, Villard once wrote that if he were dictator he would "muster out the fleet . . . and reduce the army to a police force of 25,000 . . . retire every single one of the talking generals and admirals and send them all to Guam with the direction that they put that island into 100 per cent preparedness and play at war maneuvers to their heart's content." The best insurance for small forces, Villard believed, was the abolition of compulsory universal military service, "for it was that devilish invention of the Germans which has made possible warfare on the present hideous scale, that is, the creation of 'Nations in arms.' " Villard reasoned that if compulsory military training were abolished, nations would be rendered incapable of building the military strength with which to attempt to dominate the world.

Along with the universal abandonment of compulsory military service, Villard advocated universal and total disarmament. He warned in 1918 of the danger of "trifling"

with the issue of disarmament by sanctioning partial or gradual disablement of military forces. He paralleled partial disarmament with partial emancipation of slaves and gradual
prohibition of alcohol:

> The danger of trifling with this issue, of talking *partial*
> disarmament, is comparable to the discussions of a partial
> freeing of the American slave by purchase or other-
> wise . . . . If there is to be partial disarmament, we shall
> simply be confronted with the old fears which have built
> up nations in arms and placed the power to make war not
> in the hands of parliaments or of peoples, but in those of
> irresponsible sovereigns and still more irresponsible cliques
> of military men. Gradual disarmament appeals no more
> than gradual prohibition or the curing of the habitual
> drunkard by limiting him to one spree a week.

In 1931, Villard, viewing Rumania's fear of Russia, Russia's fear of all capitalistic nations, and French fears of Germany and Italy, was more than ever convinced that only
total disarmament could forestall another war. Thus convinced, it was only natural that Villard was vitally interested
in the disarmament conferences of the twenties and early
thirties, the results of which he found for the most part inadequate. Villard welcomed the opening of the Washington
Conference of 1921 and 1922 at which the Secretary of State,
Charles Evans Hughes, made it clear that the United States
favored immediate action on disarmament. In Villard's view,
a "great beginning" had been made: "We have set up a
standard for all sincere men to repair to and it will seem so
reasonable and sensible, so generous and wise to the plain

people everywhere and particularly in America that the diplomats must come to it."

Secretary of State Hughes offered the conference a three-point plan for restriction of the navies of the United States, Great Britain, and Japan. He proposed that all programs for the building of more capital ships be abandoned for a ten-year period; a large number of battleships of older types still in commission be scrapped; and that the remaining tonnage of battleships, and also of smaller fighting craft, be fixed in a ratio of 5–5–3 for the United States, Great Britain, and Japan respectively. His program called for the destruction of some thirty vessels with a tonnage of more than 840,000 by the United States, of nineteen vessels with a tonnage of 449,000 by Great Britain, and of seventeen vessels with a tonnage of 449,000 by Japan. The Japanese protested that the ratio properly should be 10–10–7 but finally yielded after the United States promised that it would refrain from increasing its fortifications of Pacific Islands. France and Italy, who had been left out of the first discussions of naval limitation, agreed after much protest to accept a ratio figure of 1.67 for capital ships but refused to permit any limitation whatever to be placed upon cruisers of less than 10,000 tons, upon destroyers and submarines, or upon aircraft. A British proposal to abolish submarines completely was counteracted by Secretary Hughes with the suggestion that the United States and Great Britain be limited to 60,000 tons of submarines each and France and Japan to 31,500 tons each. These ideas, however, were not adopted. An attempt on the part of the United States to include the reduction of land armaments in the program of the conference was defeated by French delegates.

Villard was disappointed on a number of grounds with the conference and the Five-Power Naval Treaty which emanated from it. Limitation of arms was agreed upon rather than their complete abandonment, and thus the conference could be "nothing more than the merest beginning of disarmament." Limitation was applied only to naval armaments and did not include land arms. The use of submarines was not outlawed. Furthermore, United States acceptance of a limitation rather than complete abandonment as urged by Britain was to Villard one of the "saddest and most discouraging things." Villard was convinced that the outcome of the conference was shaped in part by the attendance and participation of military experts. With resignation, Villard commented with reference to military and naval experts, "The question is whether we are not asking too much of any professional man to request that he take part in the whittling down of his own trade with the belief openly expressed that these first steps will lead eventually to the abolition of the entire profession." The Japanese compromise and French demands proved to Villard that the delegates of those two nations did not really contemplate peace but maneuvered for "reduced and more highly efficient instruments of war."

On the other hand, Villard did not evaluate the conference as a complete failure. He recognized that it did result in a definite limitation of naval armaments—"Perhaps only the first step," he wrote, "but for every advance in the right direction at a time when the whole world seems bent on suicide we give thanks with full and grateful hearts." Villard also credited the conference with performing the service of educating the public. "The Conference," he explained, "cannot be merely a ghastly joke because of the enormous educational value it has had, because of the revelation of themselves and their methods which the diplomats have given before the onlooking world." But more important in Villard's view was the part the conference played in influencing public opinion in favor of disarmament:

> Now few dare seriously to urge that universal military service and complete preparedness, which it was the pose to advocate only a few years ago. Disarmament is the fashion once more. Disappointed as liberals must be that the Conference has achieved no more, that it has left land armaments wholly untouched, and that it has failed to scrap all naval armaments as it could so easily have done, let it be written down in truth that here in America it has helped to reverse the current of popular feeling.

In 1927 the United States invited the signatories to the Five-Power Naval Treaty to a second conference at Geneva for the purpose of extending its provisions to restrictions on smaller naval armaments. This conference accomplished little, primarily because the United States, Great Britain, and Japan could not find a satisfactory basis of agreement in their search for a formula to extend restrictions on naval arms. Villard was again critical of the reliance on military advisors at disarmament conferences. "It is unfortunate," he said in 1927, "that the 'experts'—military and naval men—are called upon in these conferences to take part in the abolition of their own careers and professions."

The London Naval Conference of 1930 continued the policy of limited naval armaments based on capital ships and aircraft carriers on the 5–5–3 ratio among the United States, Great Britain, and Japan, and for Class *A* cruisers on a 6–5–4 ratio. While the number of Class *B* cruisers, destroyers, and submarines allowed each power was not specified, tonnage for each power was limited. Thus the conference attempted to bring to a halt uncontrolled competition in building among the leading naval powers. To Villard the concept of limitation of armaments was far from satisfactory. He persisted in his demands for complete disarmament and by 1932 was urging that the United States follow such a course alone if need be.

Because he was convinced that military force, coercion, and war had never proved satisfactory solutions to international problems, Villard considered the existence and maintenance of a military machine an unnecessary and costly burden. Furthermore, it contributed to an atmosphere of fear and distrust within which the conduct of international relations could only be strained and nations on the defensive. Villard envisioned a better world—one in which there would be mutual respect, confidence, trust, and cooperation among nations; one in which the problems of nations could be composed and adjudicated by international tribunals, thus rendering wars obsolete. It is to a consideration of these other aspects of Villard's internationalism that the remaining pages of this chapter are devoted.

Alternatives to war as a method of resolving disputes among nations may be classified under two headings, namely those which are political in essence and those which are of a judicial nature. Included among the former are, for example, conciliation and conference; among the latter, arbitration and submission to a permanent international tribunal. Utterly opposed as he was to the use of force, it was natural

that Oswald Garrison Villard should support these more
rational methods of dealing with international problems.

International conference is the joint consideration and discussion by representatives of two or more nations of matters
of common interest. Historically, it has been difficult to
secure international conference where, and especially when,
it was needed. In part to meet that defect, the concept
evolved of a permanent organization to provide ever-ready
conference machinery in times of international crisis and to
provide a forum within which the day-to-day problems of
common interest to nations could be worked out cooperatively. In this sense the League of Nations in the twenties
and the present United Nations may be viewed in the nature
of mechanisms for permanent and continuous international
conference.

Oswald Garrison Villard recognized conference as a
proper method of international relations. On numerous occasions he displayed his faith in the method by calling for
international conferences on particular issues. Characteristic
was his call for a conference to take steps to end the world-
wide economic crisis following the stock market crash of
1929. At that time Villard wrote in part as follows:

> [The problems of Europe] can be conquered only by
> International action and cooperation . . . . Why are the
> nations not working together, through their rulers? Why
> are the latter not meeting like the executives of a great en-
> dangered bank, if only to get to know one another, if only
> to exchange views, to plan for united action and a united
> front? One of the best-known diplomats in London de-
> clared not long ago that he had never been able to see why

the rulers were not meeting for just this purpose. It is an international problem, he said, not a national one, and can be solved only by men with authority sitting in almost continuous session.

As early as 1916, the *Nation* had taken a position in favor of a continuous international organization dedicated to unremitting efforts to maintain peace throughout the world. In 1918 and throughout the 1920's the *Nation*, under Villard's leadership, was to reassert and maintain that position.

Villard also had certain convictions about the manner in which conferences should be conducted. One of these concerned open diplomacy. Because of the rather widespread belief that the First World War was caused in considerable measure by the secret maneuvers of diplomats, the first of Woodrow Wilson's Fourteen Points had called for "open covenants of peace, openly arrived at, after which there shall be no private international understandings of any kind, but diplomacy shall proceed always frankly and in the public view." The rationale behind such a provision was that if covenants were open, the moral force of public opinion could be brought to bear on agreements among nations which might tend to destroy the peace.

Yet the most important issues of the Peace Conference at Paris which followed the end of hostilities in 1918 were discussed behind closed doors and by a handful of men. Villard was bitterly disappointed, convinced as he was that the conference should be conducted with full publicity.

The peace conference opened on January 18, 1919. Exactly one week later, on January 25, 1919, the *Nation* published its first dispatch direct from the conference, which was being covered by Villard himself. Already President Wilson had conceded the first of his Fourteen Points. A preliminary council had decided that the real work of the conference would be executed in secret meetings. Villard was appalled. He feared first that Wilson's willingness to compromise on this issue was an indication that he might compromise on others; second, he argued that open diplomacy was a crucial necessity if Wilson was to retain the support of public opinion which was vital to the achievement of his other objectives:

> The preliminary council [decided] to make utter mockery of Wilson's avowal of open covenants of peace openly arrived at, . . . How the President could have yielded on this vital point is absolutely inconceivable for it is fundamental, and essential to victory on other issues. His one hope of success lies in securing the continued support of public sentiment by letting the peoples who have so warmly acclaimed him since his arrival in Europe know just what is going on, that they may stand behind him. Behind closed doors he can easily be outvoted, and without stenographic minutes all sorts of stories may be freely circulated to his injury. This is so evident that the whole fate of the conference may obviously depend upon the stand taken now. Yet President Wilson was present when the fatal action was taken, and he seems neither to have protested nor to have seen the impropriety of rules of procedure for the conference being laid down by a totally different body . . . .
>
> Wilson has thus early resumed his old habit of compromising . . . There is no bigger issue than covenants

openly arrived at, and he who starts by yielding at the beginning is likely to yield in the middle and all the way through as a result of his early weakness.

Villard continued throughout the conference to criticize what he considered press censorship and secret diplomacy. President Wilson, he concluded, evidently had "no intention of using the American press to educate people" on the terms of the peace. "The uncomfortable fact is," Villard continued, writing in February of 1919, "that the Conference is moving slowly and so much in the dark that public interest in its work may wane."

Villard was to criticize other international conferences of the twenties on the same grounds. Of the Washington Conference, for example, he wrote that "we have had neither open diplomacy nor all the publicity that is possible. There ought to be more open sessions in such a conference and more public debate . . . . If there should be a succession of such conferences, every one of them should witness more and more publicity, more and more talking and negotiating in the open."

Another aspect of conference procedure which concerned Villard was the amount of participation accorded to the members of the conference. Villard's concept of an international conference was that of a deliberative body in which all members would share in the deliberations and the policy-making with adequate debate and full publicity. In this respect also, he was destined to be disappointed in the Paris Peace Conference. Plenary sessions at which the entire membership of the conference met together were few in number. On the occasions when they did meet, little deliberation took place. They acted rather more in the nature of a ratifying agency. The important issues of the conference were resolved in smaller groups such as that in which President Wilson, President Georges Clemenceau of France, Italy's Premier Vittorio Orlando, and David Lloyd George, Prime Minister of Great Britain, made the important decisions. As early as February 1, 1919, Villard spoke of "the little inner group [President Wilson and the premiers] who seem to have usurped the functions of the conference . . . Secret covenants of peace secretly arrived at seem to be the rule with them, and one wonders whether the conference itself will ever have any other function than solemnly to ratify their action."

A few weeks later on April 26, 1919, Villard wrote with increased bitterness and an ominous note of warning about the chances for future peace:

> The very existence of this committee is the result of an arrogant, unauthorized assumption of power, for never and nowhere did the conference endow Messrs. Wilson, Orlando, Clemenceau and Lloyd George with authorization to transact all the business and come to all the decisions . . . .
>
> How is it possible to produce a democratic peace or a lasting one under such conditions? A democratic peace, frankly, it can never be; a lasting peace it can be only if heaven shows an unexampled favor.

The occasion of the Second International Conference of Socialists at Berne, Switzerland, in February of 1919, gave Villard the opportunity to compare and contrast the methods and procedures of that body with those of the Paris Peace Conference. Villard preferred the Berne Conference.

The Second or Socialist International was more democratic in membership, allowed full debate and the utmost publicity, and in general offered more hope at that time of a constructive future than did the proceedings at Paris:

> For here is a real conference, in fullest publicity, with real debating, a conference of men and women, a conference of victors and vanquished alike, . . . a conference which . . . is absolutely without official domination. Nobody in Berne is taking orders, and the gathering meets three times a day instead of twice in four weeks.
>
>   . . . . .
>
> Though no Socialist myself, if I had the power to decide on which conference to rest the future of the world, I should unhesitatingly, and with real joy decide for this simple conference with its plain membership . . . the hands of a democratic gathering of democratic people, the real representatives of those who have fought, bled and died for their countries.

From the mid-nineteenth century on, the efforts on the part of statesmen, liberals, and humanitarians to substitute the authoritative decision of impartial judges for a resort to war in the settlement of international disputes had become more vocal, articulate, and concerted. These efforts were manifested in a movement calling for greater reliance on arbitration, a means of settlement of international disputes by impartial judges on the basis of respect for law. At the Hague Peace Conferences of 1899 and 1907, arbitration was accepted as the most effective and equitable means of settling disputes. The second Hague Conference, while it did not achieve it, at least went on record as accepting in principle "compulsory" arbitration. The Hague Conferences also envisioned a permanent judicial tribunal which would further international law and promote the pacific settlement of international disputes.

Subsequently, President William Howard Taft and his Secretary of State, Philander C. Knox, negotiated treaties with Great Britain and France, providing for the arbitration of all justiciable questions, which were designed as models for future arbitration pacts. These treaties did not even except from compulsory arbitration those matters dealing with "vital interests" and "national honor" which previous agreements had contained. Unfortunately, these treaties suffered such emasculating changes by the United States Senate that President Taft refused to ratify them. In evaluating the career of Secretary of State Philander Knox, Villard took occasion to write sympathetically of Knox's attempted contributions in this area:

> He had much to be proud of . . . [He did] sign the great arbitration pacts with France and England . . . he preceded these treaties with a circular note to all the great powers asking them to set up and support an international court of arbitral justice at The Hague, to have jurisdiction of practically all questions arising between countries. He believed that the establishment of this court would reduce armaments, and he was bold enough to believe, with many pacifists, that its decrees and decisions would be carried into effect merely by the force of the enlightened public opinion of the world. He felt that the court would speedily build up a code of law applicable to all cases by its own decisions based upon the fundamental principles of international law and equity.

By 1919 and 1920 there was considerable world opinion favoring the establishment of a permanent judicial tribunal to which international differences could be referred for adjudication. Villard reflected the thoughts of many Americans when he advocated, before the end of the First World War, the establishment of an international court to which "shall be submitted all issues between nations, dropping once for all the phrase about causes which affect the honor of a nation, precisely as courts between individuals are not in the least affected by the individual honor of such of those who come before it." The idea of a world court was concretely manifested in the provision of the Covenant of the League of Nations which called for the formulation and submission to the members of plans for the establishment of a Permanent Court of International Justice. To this end a group of jurists met at The Hague in June of 1920. Villard expressed his hopes for the outcome of their deliberations. He called for a genuine world court with compulsory jurisdiction and again made a plea for an extension into the international field of the judicial remedies accorded to private individuals:

> The Third Hague Conference should call for a genuine world court by empowering the Hague Court to pass upon disputes relating to purely international matters, with power to summon into court all parties to a suit or controversy. That is, it should have obligatory jurisdiction . . . Let us sheathe the sword for all time, let us ask of nations what we expect of all human beings, that they turn from private murder to courts, let us acknowledge the complete failure of force to remake character, to instill virtue, to ennoble souls. Let us try the other way, the other means—the way that lies through Nazareth.

During the 1920's, opinion in the United States moved slowly in the direction of participation in a world court. In 1923, President Warren Harding presented the protocol embodying the international court to the United States Senate with reservations. Villard's *Nation* urged immediately that the United States accept the protocol as a step in the right direction, even though the periodical described the court as a disappointment to the extent that it retained the distinction between justiciable and nonjusticiable controversies and that it did not go far enough toward compulsory jurisdiction, codification of international law, and the outlawry of war. Although Villard opposed the League of Nations, he refused to go along with the so-called irreconcilables in the Senate (of whom his friend William E. Borah was one) who objected to the world court on the basis that it was a backdoor entrance into the league. While the Senate, led by such men as Borah and Hiram Johnson of California, delayed action for many months, the proposal for the world court gained support throughout the country. Both major political parties endorsed it, and the House of Representatives adopted a resolution expressing approval of the protocol in March of 1925. The Senate took final action on June 27, 1926, approving United States adherence to the court subject to reservations, among which was one to the effect that advisory opinions should be rendered publicly after public hearing, and opportunity for hearing given to the parties concerned, and that the court should not, without the consent of the United States, "entertain any request for an advisory opinion touching any dispute or question in which the United States has or claims an interest." [15] As late as the fall of 1929, the signa-

[15] See Charles Fenwick, *International Law* (3rd ed.; New York: Appleton-Century-Crofts, Inc., 1948), pp. 523–24.

tories to the protocol were still attempting to find a basis
of agreement with the United States over this reservation.
By this time Villard was urging that the United States participate in the world court with or without reservations.

> A more immediate constructive step is for those of us who
> believe in our adherence to the World Court with or
> without conditions, to move for our entry into that or-
> ganization. Personally it seems to me it would have been a
> great deal better had we built on the old Hague tribunal.
> I am not much interested in reservations, but I am tremen-
> dously interested in seeing a genuine World Court into
> which every nation should obligate itself to take each and
> every cause which might lead it into conflict with another
> country. But let us get on with the experiment now
> offered to us, even if it be a mess of compromises.

Although the United States eventually signed the protocol,
Senate approval was never forthcoming. It was not until a
Second World War had occurred that the United States
was to join a world court.

On January 3, 1918, Oswald Garrison Villard, looking
ahead to the end of the war in Europe, urged among his
"reconstruction proposals" the establishment of a permanent
organization of nations as a partial means for the advancement of peace and of democracy. He envisioned such an organization as an "international parliament." "The time has
surely passed," argued Villard, "for either elucidating the
proposal or advancing arguments in its behalf."

Thus, when President Wilson, on January 8, 1918, advocated, among his Fourteen Points upon which the peace should be based, a general association of nations under specific covenants for affording mutual guarantees of political independence and territorial integrity to great and small states alike, Villard and his *Nation* were in accord. Yet Villard was subsequently to become one of the most vocal opponents of the Versailles Treaty which incorporated the League of Nations. As such, he found himself in company with the forces of isolation and nationalism. As described in his memoirs, it was not a situation in which he took much comfort:

> It was hard for us to oppose the League for all of us had dreamed of a parliament of man, and still harder to find ourselves fighting alongside of Boies Penrose and Henry Cabot Lodge and his satellites, but fight we did and so gave aid and comfort to those whom we opposed at every other point, whose whole influence upon our public life and social and economic progress seemed to us about the most dangerous in our politics. That had happened to us before and happened to us again; one can only stick to the chart one has chosen to sail by and not be diverted by the character of the consorts that may for a brief moment take a parallel course.[16]

Villard's primary objection to the League of Nations was that it was an integral part of the Treaty of Versailles. The League, argued Villard, was "fatally involved with the wickedness of the Treaty itself," and he considered the treaty iniquitous, to say the least. It is true, however, that Villard viewed the Covenant itself as containing some inadequacies.

[16] Villard, *Fighting Years,* p. 460.

He objected mainly to what he considered the undemocratic nature of the League in that the four or five great powers of the world were accorded the dominant position on the League Council, which was in part a policy-forming and in part an executive body. Villard feared that the council would attempt to rule the world in its own self-interest. He expressed his misgivings in a public address in 1920:

> Others, like myself, can see in the League nothing else than a device to fasten definitely upon the world the domination of the four Great Powers who controlled the Entente during the war and whose shortsighted or inhumane statesmanship is responsible for the starving of Russia, the horrors of Hungary, the wicked injustice to the Tyrol, the carving up of Central Europe so as to create not one Alsace-Lorraine but a dozen . . . We find the League as now constituted so hopelessly undemocratic in structure as to be beyond remedy. It places in the hands of a half dozen men sitting behind closed doors and entirely beyond the reach of public sentiment, particularly in an emergency, powers that no such group should ever be called upon to exercise.

Villard's real opposition to the League, however, was rooted in his fear that, instead of functioning as an institution to prevent war, the League would become chiefly an agency "to carry out the terms of the peace"—terms contained in the Treaty of Versailles of which Villard was a bitter and vocal opponent.

Even before World War I had ended, Villard began to urge a just and humane peace—a peace concluded in a spirit of forgiveness and magnanimity. He advocated use of the methods of modern penology on Germany, that she be treated in such a way that she could most quickly become a useful and full member of the society of nations. He argued that too harsh a penalty or punishment would only serve to foster animosity and to perpetuate cause for further dissension. As early as January 3, 1918, Villard was writing:

> Much will, of course, depend upon the spirit of those who have to make the new peace and to reconstruct the world. A peace signed in bitterness and hate and continued in that spirit will be of dubious duration. We ought to forgive our public enemies as readily as we forgive the individual who commits a crime against us, but there is an ethical duty for public opinion to exact proof of German recognition of wrong doing and of sincerity of conversion before the sinner should be received as one entirely cleansed of crime. The outraged public opinion of the world may certainly be counted upon to take care of this; its attitude and that of the peacemakers ought not to be that of men seeking to punish the greatest crimes in history by robbery or by the exaction of impossible penalties, but rather of the judges of modern penology, who desire to impose only that penalty which shall most speedily restore the criminal to society as a useful, safe, and worthy member.

Five days later, President Wilson appeared before Congress and delivered his famous Fourteen Points message, the provisions of which seemed to Villard to contain the basis for the just and humane peace which he desired. Wilson's subsequent war messages served to further Villard's hopes for the kind of postwar settlement envisioned by liberals throughout the world.

The Treaty of Versailles which emerged from the Peace Conference at Paris seemed to many liberals, Villard included, grossly inconsistent with Wilson's earlier proposals. The terms of the treaty provided for the return of Alsace-Lorraine to France; the permanent demilitarization and a fifteen-year occupation by Allied forces of the west bank of the Rhine River; the severe limitation of the German Army and Navy; and an Anglo-French-American treaty of mutual defense against Germany. The treaty further provided that Germany should be deprived of all of her colonial possessions and that they should become mandates of the League of Nations; that Danzig should be established as a free city; that a Polish Corridor to the Baltic should be established; and that Italy should be given a portion of the Austrian Tyrol which contained some 200,000 Germans. On the matter of reparations, the treaty was especially harsh, demanding that Germany restore all losses incurred by the Allied and associated nations, even including pensions to military victims and their families. Germany was also to deliver to Great Britain, France, and Belgium a large quantity of reparations in kind—merchant ships, livestock, coal, and various manufactured products. In Villard's view, these provisions imposed a harsh settlement and contained the seeds of future wars. He wrote to Senator Robert M. La Follette to this effect and reiterated his lack of faith in the League:

I see it is stated in the press that you are going to speak against the Treaty. I hope with all my heart that you will speak not only against the Covenant, which is such a travesty on the League of Nations we have all been hoping for, but against the Treaty itself. The more I study it, the more I am convinced that it is the most iniquitous peace document ever drawn, that it dishonors America because it violates our solemn national pledge given to the Germans at the time of the Armistice and because it reeks with bad faith, revengefulness and inhumanity. It is worse than the Treaty of Vienna. Evidently Mr. Wilson and I do not use and understand words in the same way, for when he says the Treaty constitutes a new order, my mind stands still and I doubt my sanity for, to me, it not only retains the old and vicious order of the world, but makes it worse and then puts the whole control of the situation in the hands of four or five statesmen—and, incidentally, of the International Bankers. To my mind it seals the ruin of the modern capitalistic system and constitutes a veritable Pandora's Box out of which will come evils of which we have not as yet any conception.

Reparations and the related problem of Allied war debts deserve attention here. In 1921 the Reparations Commission, created under the Treaty of Versailles, fixed Germany's reparations bill at $33,000,000,000. At this time, Allied Powers owed to the United States a total of some $10,350,-000,000 for loans advanced to them during and after the war. As early as 1919, the debtor states moved to have their debts canceled or reduced. Eventually, the United States did make arrangements by which about one half of the original principal was forgiven but refused to cancel the debts in their entirety. It soon became apparent, however, that the United

States would receive payment on the Allied debts only if Germany made reparations payments, which were proving to be too high for the German economy to bear.

A number of persons in the United States thought the debt and reparations settlements were not only ignoble but unwise. Oswald Garrison Villard repeatedly called for a new international conference to reconsider the matter. In 1924 the Dawes Plan, an attempt to redevise the reparations payments, went into effect. This plan provided that the United States and the Allies should loan Germany $200,000,000 in gold to speed up her industrial recovery and to back a new currency issue. Her reparations payments were then to be allotted in such a way that she would make progressively larger payments over the years as she improved her economic conditions. This plan, too, did not prove wholly successful, and by 1926 there was again agitation for cancellation of war debts. By this time the continued insistence of the United States that the war debts be repaid was contributing to the unpopularity of the American government abroad. Villard called attention to the situation in a *Nation* article written in London during a trip abroad and urged the cancellation of part of the war debts:

> Our debt policy plus our tariff policy and our position as money-lenders to the world are gradually forming a European alliance against America. The European nations are frightened by our tremendous financial power; they cannot borrow money elsewhere, but they are trying to find means to defend themselves against our pressure to make them pay their debts, and our refusal, by means of our high tariffs to let them pay with goods.

·   ·   ·   ·   ·

The *Nation's* policy of urging the cancellation of the debts that we shall never be able to collect and accepting funding arrangements based on capacity to pay is the correct one. I am not, of course, optimistic enough to believe that we should receive many, if any, thanks from those whom we release from indebtedness.

Villard was not so benighted as to advocate cancellation of debts with no strings attached. He argued that in return the United States should insist, among other things, on disarmament and the abolition of poison gas, submarines, and war planes. "In these inventions of the devil," he maintained, "lie not only the seeds of other wars but the genuine possibility of the complete destruction of our modern civilization."

In 1929, another attempt to arrive at a solution of the debts and reparations problems was made in the Young Plan of December 22, 1928, in which once more Germany's reparations payments were scaled down. By the time the Young Plan went into effect, the world-wide depression had set in, and in 1931 President Herbert Hoover, on re-examining the whole problem, announced a moratorium for one year during which no reparations payments or Allied debts were to be paid. Villard, who would have favored cancellation or drastic reduction of Europe's war debts, supported the moratorium and warned that debts and reparations stood in the way of the complete economic recovery of Europe:

As long as debts and reparations stand in the way, it will not be possible to rehabilitate the shattered nerves and restore to balance the psychology of Europe. Until this question is settled, the normal processes of trade cannot recur. As long as debts and reparations continue on the books of the nations, they will form a barrier to the recovery of our own country over which no tide of returning prosperity can easily flow . . . It is a fact that the payment of reparations money has been doing injury to our business life by unsettling trade in the debtor nations and introducing into it an economic factor not created by the normal processes of give and take in international barter.

It should be noted that payments on neither reparations nor war debts were ever resumed to any meaningful extent.

The expression of self-determination, or the right of a people to determine its own sovereignty, gained currency during the First World War and was given impetus by President Wilson's Fourteen Points message which specified the return of Alsace-Lorraine to France, the readjustment of the frontiers of Italy "along clearly recognizable lines of nationality," the creation of an independent Polish state, and the autonomous development of Austria-Hungary and of the foreign nationalities under Turkish rule. Many liberals joined President Wilson in viewing self-determination as a necessary and proper basis for a just and permanent peace. Writing in the *Nation* prior to the Fourteen Points address, Villard had urged the acceptance of "Abraham Lincoln's immortal saying that no man is good enough to govern any other man without that other man's consent as the only sound guiding principle for the readjustment of national, international, and racial relationships." Villard was convinced that one nation or people could not control another without the corruptibility of human nature evidencing itself. "The truth is," he said, "human nature is so weak that it is impossible to give any set of human beings control over another without their human nature going to pieces and becoming bestial. Our own American soldiers behaved very badly in the Philippines and in China, and so do the troops of any other nation."

By 1921, Villard was calling attention to the awakening nationalism of such areas as the Philippines, India, and Korea. He interpreted it as a logical extension of the struggle for individual self-expression, and he urged the free nations to set an example:

> In cases of this kind there is afoot a newly awakening race consciousness, or spirit of nationality if you please, which to my mind is of the profoundest significance and value. As the individual, the world over, is being taught that complete self-expression is the highest aim, so these struggling groups are likewise seeking to obtain their highest group self-expression. The only question is how, when nationality is achieved, it can be guided in the right paths to respect the rights of all others. The answer is certainly that we cannot expect it to follow them unless the great nations who so doubt the capacity for self-government of the struggling ones can themselves set a just and honorable example, can refrain from themselves exploiting Haiti, Santo Domingo, India, and Korea and Egypt and Tripoli and all the rest now enslaved.

Villard was not impressed with the argument that these backward peoples had to be prepared for self-government. He argued that a nation could only obtain self-government by practicing it. Addressing the India Society in 1925, he said:

A nation can only attain self-government by practicing self-government . . . a backward nation must have the right to climb to sound self-government by stumbling and falling, not once, but many times, . . .

I think the world needs nothing so much today as to see the Indian peoples set themselves to the task of self-government however great and terrible the odds with which they must contend . . . the world needs nothing so much as some of these experiments in self-government because faith in democracy and democracy itself are at a low ebb . . . .

In Egypt, India, China, South Africa, the Philippines . . . there are stirrings to challenge the existing order . . . I welcome these tests, I welcome these conflicts, for I believe with all my heart that out of them will come a purification, a clearing of the atmosphere, a driving out of our national lives of endless humbugs and hypocrisy.

Villard's hope was that India's gaining of independence from Britain would encourage other colonial peoples to strive for their freedom. He expressed this view in a letter to D. S. Chang, editor of the Seoul, Korea, daily *Dong Ah Ilbo*, on the occasion of its tenth anniversary:

May I also extend to your paper on this tenth anniversary the heartiest greetings of *The Nation*, which since 1865 has been devoting itself to the liberties of minorities, the right of all peoples to their own way of life, and to opposition to imperialism from whatever source?

In view of this I need hardly assure you of our interest in the causes championed by the distinguished newspaper which you represent. We have never faltered in our belief that the Koreans were entitled to their own independent existence, precisely as we have violently opposed the imperialistic moves of our own country in Nicaragua, Haiti and elsewhere . . . . If India now throws off the shackles of English rule, enslaved people everywhere will be heartened to strike off their own shackles. We are even hopeful that the present American Congress will this year grant unconditional freedom to the Filipinos, something that we of *The Nation* have been asking for ever since our fleet sailed into Manila harbor on May 1, 1898.

The unfortunate result of Villard's letter to Mr. Chang, however, was the suspension of *Dong Ah Ilbo* by the Japanese authorities on the ground that Villard's letter, reprinted in its columns, was "inciting."

Villard's most direct effort on behalf of self-determination during the twenties, and one which he described as bringing "a torrent of abuse" down upon the *Nation* and its editors, was one on behalf of Irish independence. While Great Britain in the early postwar years was formulating Home Rule plans for Ireland, the Irish themselves, given impetus by President Wilson's advocacy of self-determination, had established a framework for independent government, and Eamon de Valera claimed the Presidency of the so-called Irish Republic. Resistance to British rule on the part of the Irish and the counter-resistance of the British led to the so-called Anglo-Irish War of 1919–21. The British use of mercenaries, the Black and Tans, and their reliance on terrorism to put down the Irish drew criticism throughout the world and, of particular importance here, from Americans of Irish background.

Irish-Americans had long supported the nationalist aspirations of their homeland, and a delegation of Irish-Americans had even gone so far as to call upon the Peace Conference at Paris to recognize the right of the Irish to self-determination, without interference from any other country. Indeed Irish-American opinion, frustrated in these attempts, was later to be influential in defeating the League of Nations.

The methods of the British Black and Tans against the Irish deeply shocked Oswald Garrison Villard, whose adherence to self-determination naturally inclined him to sympathy with the Irish cause. It seems reasonable to assume, too, that he was influenced by his Irish friends among his fellow liberals. For example, Frank P. Walsh, a prominent labor lawyer, who was associated with Villard in many liberal causes, was one of those who appeared in Paris on behalf of de Valera.

It was at the suggestion of a young Irish doctor, residing in New York City, that Villard and his *Nation* in the fall of 1929 moved to establish a committee of one hundred citizens to make a study of conditions in Ireland. Professor Robert Morss Lovett and Jane Addams were among those liberals who responded. In a letter to a British subscriber to the *Nation*, Villard explained the rationale upon which the committee was established. His concern, he stated, was for the effect the aroused passions of Irish-Americans might have on American politics and the danger of war with Great Britain which he felt was inherent in the situation:

> I am so glad that you like The Nation and hope that you have been sympathetic with our effort, however mad a venture it may seem toward the solution of the Irish problem. The truth is that the situation is becoming very alarming on this side. The Irish people are being inflamed, as the New York riots show, by the news of the suffering and deaths among their relatives. The danger is, too, that it will

drift into politics. I am afraid that the plight of Ireland will be discussed in our Congress with a great deal of vehemence and bitterness. A powerful group has just been formed to compel Congres to recognize the independence of Ireland. Some of our best authorities believe that there is a grave possibility that war with England may loom up unless the situation is speedily relieved; hence, we thought that we could not remain silent and we hoped that our committee might at least act as a safety-valve. It is by no means clear, however, just what we can accomplish.

Although Villard and the *Nation* staff were the prime movers behind the Citizen's Committee of One Hundred, Villard claimed that the official relationship of the *Nation* ceased at the point at which the committee selected a group of five persons to assume leadership. This group, which was later enlarged, became known as the American Commission on Conditions in Ireland. Villard attempted to clarify the apparent confusion over names to the managing editor of the *New York Times:*

It is true that the newspapers have varying names for the Irish Commission, the exact title of which is the American Commission on Conditions in Ireland. I regret that the Commission saw fit to prefix the word "American," as that has given rise to the mis-understanding that it is perhaps official, but with that designation I had nothing to do. My relation to the Commission has been limited solely to calling into being the Committee of 100 and not the Commission as you suggest. That Commission, originally of five, was elected by two votes of the Committee. I have scrupulously kept away from the meetings of the Commission, except on two occasions when I was present as a spectator, in order that the Commission should feel perfectly free to act without regard to my views in the matter.

In November of 1920, the Commission on Conditions in Ireland announced a subcommittee which was to go to Ireland to conduct an on-the-spot investigation. The subcommittee was cautioned not to overlook the British point of view and to tap official government sources of information as well as to elicit all shades of public opinion. The subcommittee's journey, however, was never realized, for the British refused to grant them visas.

Meanwhile the commission proceeded to pursue its investigations in the United States, establishing its base of operations in Washington, D.C. The commission, now chaired by Jane Addams and consisting of Senators David I. Walsh and George Norris, L. Hollingsworth Wood, Frederic C. Howe, James H. Maurer, Norman Thomas, and Major Oliver P. Newman, remained in session for weeks and heard numerous witnesses.

Irish-Americans, encouraged by the resulting publicity and sympathy attendant to the situation in Ireland and the American response, became more impassioned in their pleas for action against the British. One speaker went so far as to urge in an address given at Madison Square Garden that the "Irish should start a race vendetta in America, take an eye for an eye and a tooth for a tooth and tear down anything English in America" if British warfare against the Irish did not stop.[17] Villard was quick to condemn this type of program. In a letter to the speaker which he made public, Villard insisted that American concern in the Irish question was only

[17] *New York Times*, Jan. 8, 1921, p. 2, col. 7.

in the interest of self-determination and was not anti-British and that violence on the part of the Irish in America would only be resented and detrimental to the Irish cause:

> America, because of its love of liberty, is bound to take a friendly interest in the struggle of any people for the control of their Government but any suggestion that the struggle be transferred to this side of the ocean will be resented throughout this country by all right-thinking Americans.
>
> Do not make any mistake; American interest in self-determination for Ireland does not imply hostility to England. Those of us here who have been most warmly urging an early solution of the Irish trouble do so primarily because we are interested in keeping the peace between England and the United States.[18]

This statement by Villard came at a time when he and his *Nation* were undergoing much criticism for their part in the Irish investigations. They were accused by some of intervening in the affairs of Britain, of encouraging the Sinn Fein organization by promoting its American propaganda, and of fostering an anti-British campaign in America. That Villard had raised fears concerning the extent to which he was willing to carry his activities on behalf of the Irish is reflected in an editorial in the *New York Times* welcoming Villard's statement quoted above:

> Apprehensions as to how far Oswald Garrison Villard might go in service of the Sinn Fein organization in promoting its American propaganda and in helping its leaders to spread here the impression that the severities practiced

[18] *Ibid.*

in Ireland by the British government are explicable only as illustrative of British cruelty and hate, now can be, not altogether dismissed, perhaps, but certainly much allayed.

For Mr. Villard does draw a line, broad and clear, enough to be clearly seen, beyond which he will not accompany the Irish revolters.

He draws it this side of starting, or even trying to start in the United States, the sort of campaign which when proposed and urged by the man Boland received vehement applause.[19]

Villard himself professed never to understand fully why the work of the Irish Commission aroused so much opposition. He commented in his memoirs that "it is hard for me to understand why that Irish Commission roused such passionate anger among the ruling classes, especially the 'society people' in New York, Boston, and Washington. I suppose that we were then still so near to the war that it seemed an effort to reflect upon the British who were still our dearly beloved Allies." [20]

The commission eventually published its report but had to admit severe limitations. The British, as might be expected, had refused to cooperate, so that the only witnesses to appear were biased in favor of the Irish. Being confined to conducting its investigations within the borders of the United States was, of course, a handicap of the first magnitude. Villard described the disadvantages under which the commission had labored to British journalist Herbert W. Horwill and admitted the failure of the commission:

[19] *Ibid.*, Jan. 10, 1921, p. 10, col. 5.
[20] Villard, *Fighting Years*, p. 487.

Our Irish Commission has concluded its hearings and has drafted a report which must necessarily be one-sided, I fear. It was practically hamstrung from the first by the refusal of your Government to let us come over and of the British witnesses, who had accepted, to keep their promises to come to this country. The Commission has also aroused extreme antagonism among well-to-do classes who do not understand and who think that we are trying to stir up trouble between England and this country . . . the undertaking has hindered rather than aided The Nation, to say nothing of the cause of freedom.

On another occasion Villard wrote apologetically to Jane Addams for having drawn her into the commission, and he spoke with disappointment of the manner in which the work of the commission had evolved: "I have felt at times utterly sick about it, the weakness of its direction and the mistakes of which we of the Nation as well as others were guilty, and so I have often reproached myself for ever having asked you to join. Nothing I have ever done has focussed such social pressure and intolerance upon us as this."

Yet in attempting to evaluate the commission in retrospect, Villard was confident that it had been helpful in diverting British attention from the concept of Home Rule to a policy of independence for Ireland. In his *Fighting Years*, he pointed to the existence of the Irish Free State as a complete justification of his Irish committee. He reprinted in this volume, with considerable pride, a letter from Dr. Albert Shaw, editor of *Digest* and a former vice president of the New York Academy of Political Science, crediting the Irish Commission with having made a real con-

tribution to the cause of Irish independence. Dr. Shaw wrote
in part to Villard:

> In the concentration of American sentiment upon the
> outrageous efforts of the British government to recon-
> quer the Irish people, the most influential episode was the
> work of the American Commission on Conditions in Ire-
> land. This was a difficult undertaking, and, in the end, it
> was proved to be a remarkable achievement . . . . There
> was great reluctance in this country to take any steps that
> were displeasing to the British authorities. They were ex-
> ceedingly hostile to any American attempts to secure fair
> play for Ireland, yet, while there was widespread Amer-
> ican sympathy for the Irish people, there was also a simi-
> larly widespread reluctance to offend the British. Thus, it
> took rare courage to assume a sponsorship for an organ-
> ized American inquiry into the conditions prevailing in
> Ireland. As editor and publisher of *The Nation*, you had
> long shown your readiness to support causes, however
> unpopular, when you believed that justice called for vindi-
> cation.
>
> As I have re-studied the events and circumstances of
> that period, I have become increasingly convinced that
> your courage in accepting suggestions that you, personally,
> and *The Nation*, as an influential journal, should initiate this
> American Commission, contributed the essential factor
> that turned the scales. This commission, composed of men
> and women of great influence, assembled a mass of testi-
> mony that could not be refuted. Mr. Lloyd George real-
> ized that the time had come for a truce to be followed by
> an arrangement far more favorable to Ireland than had

been proposed in the Home Rule programs of Parnell and Gladstone.[21]

Accepting the platform of New York's Progressive Party in 1925, Villard acquiesced in a plank which called not only for "self-determination for every nation, unhampered and unembarrassed under institutions of her own choosing," but which demanded recognition by the United States of every government so established. The immediate issue to which this plank was directed was the matter of nonrecognition of Russia on the part of the United States.

There are, traditionally, two rules of recognition developed through international law. The first is that a new government coming into power by extraconstitutional means should be recognized when it meets the test of being a *de facto* government; that is, when it is in actual control of the governmental machinery and is exercising its authority without substantial opposition. The second rule is that recognition should be granted if the new government is prepared to carry out the obligations of the state under international law.

The United States steadfastly refused throughout the 1920's to recognize the Soviet Union, ostensibly on the basis that the Bolshevik government had failed to recognize the debts of the Czarist regime and of the Kerensky government. There seems, however, to be considerable evidence that the United States withheld recognition because of dislike for and distrust of the political principles of the new Soviet government.

Oswald Garrison Villard repeatedly criticized the United

[21] *Ibid.*, pp. 490–91.

States policy of nonrecognition of Russia on grounds other than those recognized by international law. While insisting that he had no sympathy for communism, he could not tolerate the rejection of Russia on the basis of disliking the form of her institutions:

> I am in favor of the immediate recognition of the Soviet government of Russia. I am entirely out of sympathy with the present use of the power of recognition as wielded in Washington. It is one of the worst things that Mr. Wilson did to institute the modern idea that recognition of a foreign government is an ethical weapon—something to be given or withdrawn, as the case may be, according to whether we like or dislike the particular government with which we happen to be dealing at the moment. I believe in the historical American policy that any established *de facto* government is entitled to recognition without reference to its morals or methods at home. Personally I do not happen to like the Communist government, I am still a Democrat and opposed to government by oligarchy, or a party or a group upheld by a Cheka, and the terrorism of dictators, but my dislike of that government has nothing to do with the question of recognition. Russia is in the family of nations and should be recognized.

Not until Woodrow Wilson and Mexico, argued Villard, did the United States "officially begin the procedure of recognition as a means of approval or disapproval or, as in the case of Mexico, as a weapon actually to over-throw the status quo."

On another occasion, Villard wrote to the effect that through the full acceptance of Russia into the family of nations she might be brought to the point of abandoning her repressive methods. "As for our own relations with Russia," he wrote, "I am more than ever convinced that we should recognize the Soviets at once and resume diplomatic relations with them . . . The sooner international relations are normal, the sooner will the force of the world's public opinion be felt here, the sooner will the Soviets reach the point where they will desist from repression and give up the punishment of those who differ from them."

Writing in 1930, Villard reiterated this view and admonished his readers against sitting in judgment on others:

> If each country is going to sit in judgment of the manners, morals and past record of every other, the world will be in for endless trouble and blood-letting. Practically no country, certainly not the United States, can come into court with clean enough hands to be able honestly to put on the judicial ermine. Finally, in numerous countries—the United States for instance—any given administration is a political one which cannot be trusted to be unaffected by purely political considerations, such as the voice of organized labor, or of organized big business.

Villard was firmly of the opinion that no country had the right to intervene in the affairs of any other country. The Russians, he argued, ought to be left to work out their own political and social problems without interference from outside. He viewed activities in Russia as an experiment, and he tended to sympathize with them as such. More than once he made a plea for patience in viewing the changes in Russia, to allow adequate time for a fair evaluation of their consequences. Upon visiting Russia in the fall of 1929, Villard reported that the Russian government had definite aims and objectives in mind and that it was not to be underrated. He rightfully predicted that if that government survived until 1933 it would be permanently entrenched:

> There can be no doubt as to the ability, the zeal and the industry of the men who constitute the present government of Russia. They impressed all by their ability, their polish, their vigor and their knowledge of what was going on outside Russia. They have a very clear vision of what they wish to achieve and how they propose to accomplish it, and very great confidence in their ability to do their job well . . . The alternative to the Soviet government, however, is anarchy and perhaps the breaking up of Russia into many States. There is not now, I repeat, the slightest chance of this taking place. The best American observers in Russia feel that if the Bolsheviki can weather the next four years without a national catastrophe, such as famine or war, they will be in the saddle beyond any possibility of unseating.[22]

Yet Villard, while sympathizing with Russian aims and objectives, was severely critical of the methods Russia was utilizing in her attempts to achieve those objectives:

> No one who has witnessed this Russian experiment and sensed its significance can remain unmoved by the human elements involved and by its dramatic quality. The deeper, therefore, the regret that the men who are doing these titanic things are savagely crushing their critics or opponents, are shooting, imprisoning, and exiling precisely as

[22] *New York Times*, Sept. 9, 1929, p. 6, col. 3.

did the Czar. The whole world yearns for a state which should really be controlled by the masses and not by handfuls of men temporarily in control of powers no group of mortals should have. Yet the Bolsheviks, with all their desire for peace, justice, liberty, and equality for a nation of workers, offer, side by side with tremendous benefits, the methods of a Caesar, a Cromwell, a Franz Josef, a Nicholas, and a Mussolini.

In spite of his disapproval of her methods, Villard was persistent in his opinion that Russia should be given "every opportunity to try out Communism to the nth degree." "I'd do anything," continued Villard, "to help them in power until they work out the changes now necessary in Russian life. This is wisdom and common sense." If the experiment failed, he suggested, the world could then "cross off communism" as unfeasible, and, too, one could not help sympathizing with the objectives of the Russian leaders. Comparing the Russian regime with that of Mussolini in Italy, Villard had no difficulty in choosing that of Russia as the more acceptable to liberals:

They [the Russian leaders] are on their way. By means of dictatorial powers, by force, by the use of exiling and drastic executions, by the use of all the means of repression to which Mussolini also resorts so freely and so basely. But with this difference: the Bolsheviks are working for the good of the masses of the working people. Their great aim is to give them vast opportunities for work, to give them clothes, tools, the leisure for rest and culture, the use of modern inventions, education; they seek to uplift them. Mussolini seeks nothing but the development of a new imperial Power in Europe, the increase of the nationalistic spirit, the further entrenchment of capitalism, of industrialism, of militarism, of government for and by the few who are privileged. No sincere democrat, no progressive, no humanitarian can fail to prefer the Russian experiment of the two autocracies, however much he may dissent from its cruelties and its intolerance.

But Villard was careful to place himself among the dissenters and to declare his faith in American democratic principles: "I, for one, cannot yet give up my faith in democracy and the liberal principles which, however often they may be honored in the breach in America, were intended to control and shape our American life." Villard had no fear of communism; he was confident that American democracy could be so strengthened as to prove without question its superiority over the Russian governmental system:

> I should not be afraid of Communism because I should set out really to constitute an honest and efficient government for the United States, one responding to the will of the American people as expressed through the initiative and referendum . . . our own system of government as reconstituted would not only challenge comparison with the Soviet program, but would seem infinitely more desirable so long as the Soviet Government is a bloody-handed class dictatorship.

That same concern for small nations, reflected in Villard's advocacy of self-determination, motivated him to oppose economic imperialism or the policy of attaining power over a nation through control of its finances. Villard was an insistent critic of United States policy toward Mexico, Honduras, Nicaragua, Venezuela, the Dominican Republic, and Haiti. Villard's concern for the problems of Haiti are of particular importance here. Perhaps, in part because of his sympathy for the colored peoples and in part motivated by his bitter disappointment in President Wilson's liberalism, Villard took up the cudgels on behalf of Haiti in the twenties.

Political instability in Haiti had led President Wilson, fearful that Germany or some other belligerent would attempt to get a foothold there and because American lives and property were threatened, to order marines to Haiti in 1914, an occupation which was to continue until 1934, and one in which Haitian finances went into American receivership. It should be noted that Amerian marines also occupied the Dominican Republic from 1916 until 1924 while its finances, too, went into American receivership. Oswald Garrison Villard labeled United States policy in these instances one of "polite conquest."

American occupation of Haiti did not proceed smoothly, and in the course of events there American marines killed some two thousand inhabitants. Villard charged that the United States then proceeded to institute authoritarian rule in both countries—all for the "sake of the dollar":

More than half the trouble in the world today is due to this invasion of the backward countries of the earth by dollar diplomacy, and . . . with the dollar inevitably comes corruption, the theft of government from the backward people, and the subjecting of them to the control of foreign conquerors—conquerors either by the dollar or the sword and usually by both. Santo Domingo is the clearest illustration of this. We went in to help and to aid in the administration of the customs. We have wound up by pulling down the government, and enforcing our rule throughout the country contrary to the wishes of the people, with no more moral right to do so than the Germans had the day they crossed the Belgian boundary.

Villard's keen and active interest in the Haitian situation is reflected in an exchange of correspondence with Senator William E. Borah in the spring and summer of 1921. Villard wrote to Borah in May of 1921 on behalf of a delegation from Haiti which wished to present its case in Washington. Villard wrote as follows:

I want earnestly to enlist your active cooperation in the matter of the three delegates of the Haitian Patriotic Union who are going to Washington the latter part of this week to present a long memoir to the Department of State (if they can secure an audience) and to the Senate Foreign Relations Committee. This memoir, which rehearses the entire story of the American occupation, is a most damning indictment of everything the Americans have done, although it is written in the most temperate kind of way. The memoir more than confirms all of the gravest charges that have been made about the military and civil occupation and adduces still others.

I earnestly hope that you will do all you can to remove the stain from the American escutcheon.

Senator Borah replied that he would be happy to receive the Haitian delegation, although he expressed doubt about the effectiveness of aid he could give. "I do not know whether, under the present regime," he wrote, "Senators will

be permitted to have any views upon the question or not."
Borah added facetiously, "Possibly I may form some in
secret at any rate." [23]

Villard was insistent that Borah initiate some kind of action but warned him that the State Department would be
opposed to congressional investigation of the matter:

> This issue fundamentally involves America's good name
> and traditions and it is highly important that the whole
> subject be aired by a thorough Congressional inquiry. But
> strong and sinister forces are at work to prevent this, to
> issue counter-propaganda to discredit the Haitians, and to
> whitewash our glaring misdeeds in both Santo Domingo
> and Haiti. The State Department apparently is seeing no
> light, for Mr. Hughes refused to see the Haitian Delegates.
> It was indirectly conveyed to them that they could not be
> received because they did not officially represent the
> Haitian government. This, of course, is mere camouflage,
> not to say hypocrisy, for although this is technically so—
> the only Haitian government being a dummy affair created
> and upheld by the bayonets of the Marine Corps and do-
> ing its bidding—any real desire to right this grievous
> wrong would have led Mr. Hughes to lend a sympathetic
> ear.[24]

By the end of June, 1928, events in Haiti had taken such
a turn for the worse that Villard persisted in urging Senator
Borah to support a congressional investigation:

[23] Letter of William E. Borah to Oswald Garrison Villard,
May 4, 1921, in William E. Borah Papers (Library of Congress,
Washington, D.C.), Box 202.

[24] Villard to Borah, May 27, 1921, Borah Papers, Box 202.

Now word comes, following the re-establishment of the censorship, that two editors have been sentenced to six months in jail and $300 fine. Their offense seems to be chiefly to have carried at the top of their paper an appeal to President Harding to withdraw the occupation forces. The murder of Lifschitz also demands clearing up—it will never be cleared up as long as the Marines in Haiti are the sole investigators. The refusal of the Dominicans likewise to accept the absurd and enslaving terms as the price of their liberty is an indication from another quarter how far astray our Caribbean policy has been. Will you not jump into this fight and push through a congressional investigation without which we shall never be able to bring the whole truth before the world and settle this question justly and honorably? [25]

The following month saw the realization of Villard's desire for congressional action. He, himself, appeared before a Senate committee and described American intervention in Haiti and Santo Domingo as the "blackest chapter in American history in the Caribbean," and, speaking on behalf of the Union Patriotique of Haiti, the National Association for the Advancement of Colored People, and the Santo Domingo Independence Society, Villard urged a special Senate investigation of conditions there. A subsequent commission under the leadership of Senator Medill McCormick (Republican, Illinois) eventually issued a report which Villard viewed as somewhat innocuous.

In 1929, President Hoover asked Congress to establish a commission to be sent to Haiti to conduct an investigation of the feasibility of withdrawal of troops from that coun-

[25] Villard to Borah, June 28, 1921, Borah Papers, Box 202.

try. Such a commission was appointed and, chaired by W. Cameron Forbes, former Governor General of the Philippines, visited Haiti in 1930. (Villard's close friend, journalist William Allen White, was a member of the Commission.) Villard expressed his delight at the appointment of the commission in a letter to Secretary of State Henry L. Stimson, written on December 17, 1929, before the commission left for Haiti: "I need hardly tell you how thankful some of us are that at last something is going to be done to end the intolerable conditions in Haiti which have failed entirely on the constructive side so far as fitting the Haitians themselves for self-government is concerned. Certainly nothing should delay the removal of our military government and the substitution of civilian authority."

The commission's final report concluded that there had been little effort during the years of American occupancy to prepare the Haitians for self-government, apparently because of an assumption on the part of the military government that the occupation would continue indefinitely. The report recommended the replacement of the military high commissioner by a civilian, the gradual withdrawal of United States troops, the preparation of the Haitians for self-government, and the election of a new President by the Haitian legislature.

Villard was more than pleased with the commission's report, as he wrote William Allen White: "You have certainly done a wonderful job and we are all thrilled by it. It gives one renewed faith that the old America will come back and our sorely tarnished idealism be restored." [26]

[26] Letter from Oswald Garrison Villard to William Allen White, March 26, 1930, in William Allen White Papers (Library of Congress, Washington, D.C.), Box 124.

Throughout the twenties, Villard criticized what he termed the government's policy of helping bankers and capitalists to exploit weaker countries—especially those of Latin America—by supporting their loans and investments with the use of military force. Villard is reported to have said that if that policy were continued "it would push all twenty of the Latin-American republics under the economic vassalage of the United States and menace the peace and prosperity of the whole western hemisphere." [27] Villard posited that the proper course for the government to follow was to serve notice on American bankers and investors that they went abroad at their own risk, that the American fleet did not follow the American bankers, and that the military forces of the United States could not be used to collect private debts. The New York Progressive Party, in which Villard was active, in 1925 stood opposed to the "use of the army and navy for the collection of either principal or interest on American investments abroad." In 1929 in a public address Villard maintained that most American liberals "want the Dwight Morrow methods of treating Mexico applied to all of Central America, and not the Marine method. They are opposed to . . . the doctrine that the flag follows the dollar, and that every American dollar invested abroad, whether honest or dishonest, is to be safeguarded by American lives."

The principles upon which Oswald Villard lived and worked have been accurately stated as "to be opposed to war, to hold no hate for any people, to be determined to champion a better world; to believe in the equality of all men and women; and to be opposed to all tyrants and all

[27] *New York Times*, Aug. 27, 1924, p. 19, col. 1.

suppression of liberty of conscience and beliefs." [28] These principles are consistent with the underlying concepts of American liberalism. They form the basis of Villard's views on foreign relations. As such, they represent an attempt to extend American liberal principles into the international sphere.

[28] *Current Biography, 1940* (New York: H. W. Wilson Co., 1940), p. 830.

CHAPTER IX

Last of the Liberals?

AN ANALYSIS OF the writings and activities of Oswald Garrison Villard demonstrates, contrary to the opinion held by some scholars, that recent American liberalism has lacked neither consistency nor continuity.

Fundamentally humanistic, American liberalism has embodied individualism, rationalism, libertarianism, and humanitarianism. In its practical application of those values, it has demanded a positive program of governmental action to provide the economic, political, and social conditions necessary to their maximum development and realization by the average man. To this end, the American liberal movements from the days of William Jennings Bryan to those of Franklin D. Roosevelt have waged war against the inequities of the economic system, have demanded new and more effective means of popular political control, and have insisted on the protection and enlargement of individual liberties. Common to them all have been beliefs that the life of the common man could be transformed, that the economic system could be brought under effective control, and that collective action was a proper means to those ends.

It is not argued that there was any one *unified* progressive or liberal movement in America—any one movement that advanced steadily toward its particular objectives with only occasional setbacks. Rather, it is contended that the various liberal movements in American social history show a consistency in their philosophic underpinnings and in their reliance on collective action through the intervention of popularly controlled government to meet contemporary problems, and that the consistency is due, in part at least, to the fact that, even in a period of severe retrogression, the liberal philosophy and spirit survived and left an indelible mark on the evolution of American liberalism. In short, there was continuity and consistency in the American liberal movement in spite of the fact that that movement was not a single, unified one.

The most marked lapse in the steady development of liberalism from 1870 to 1932 was that which characterized the 1920's. Yet that period cannot be isolated from its past and from its future. The period was not devoid of liberalism; indeed, those years provided personnel and programs which nurtured the philosophy and method of recent liberalism throughout an era which saw that movement on the wane; in reality, the period formed a link between the more concrete and articulate movements—the New Freedom and the New Deal. Oswald Garrison Villard's definition and defense of liberalism throughout the period is impressive and persuasive evidence in support of this position.

Throughout the twenties, Oswald Garrison Villard stoutly supported the traditional American liberties of freedom of thought and expression and sought to enlarge the scope of criminal justice. He crusaded zealously and faithfully to extend individual rights and equal opportunity and protection to minority and underprivileged groups.

Villard campaigned continuously and vigorously on behalf of political democracy, his efforts directed at the attainment of more responsive and more responsible political institutions—more popularly controlled government. Not content with this alone, Villard looked to voluntary organizations, particularly the political party, as a means of assuring opposition and minority participation in the political process and as a medium of restraint on government.

Capitalism, Villard concluded, had failed to confer adequate economic advantages on the people at large and thus was in need of modification. Such, he believed, was the task of a political authority made responsive and responsible to the people. Laissez faire, with its implication of rugged individualism, was rejected by Villard as an outmoded and inadequate economic doctrine devoted to special interests.

Villard's liberalism encompassed internationalism; his concern for the human individual was a concern for all mankind. His belief in freedom led him to accept wholeheartedly the doctrine of self-determination of nations. His concern for the release of the individual from economic bondage was extended to embrace a determined opposition to economic imperialism. His faith in the rationality of mankind had a logical extension in his faith that international problems could be resolved cooperatively and peacefully rather than through force.

Villard's was a pragmatic approach to social institutions, an approach which led him to advocate experimentation and the rejection or modification of those institutions which proved ineffective in meeting human needs. The underlying assumption of his pragmatism was a belief that the social environment could be brought under social control and that social changes could be more effectively guided by collective social action than by tradition or reliance on some "invisible hand."

In the fourteen years of Villard's complete control of the *Nation*, he and his staff were dedicated to the perpetuation of principles representative of the best in American liberalism. Individualism, rationalism, pragmatism, libertarianism, and humanitarianism; pacifism, anti-imperialism, and internationalism; tolerance and social engineering—Oswald Garrison Villard's writings and activities embraced them all, and together they form a kind of mosaic of recent American liberalism. Always, Villard viewed the America of his day—its social, economic, and political institutions—with both pride and protest. He looked with pride upon its achievements and did his utmost to preserve and protect them; he looked with protest upon its deficiencies and injustices and constantly exposed and attempted to eliminate them; he looked with enthusiastic optimism to a future in which its accomplishments would be consolidated and enlarged.

The task of predicting the future course of American liberalism is necessarily a precarious and pretentious one. If the period after the Second World War is contrasted with that immediately following the First World War, the casual observer would recognize that both periods were characterized by significant evidences of reaction, suspicion, and intolerance. The McCarthyism of the 1950's would seem to have had its counterpart in the Red hunt of Attorney

General A. Mitchell Palmer. The casual observer might
be tempted to conclude that, since the voices of liberalism
succeeded in surviving the twenties, there is cause to be
optimistic in calculating their chances for having survived
the fifties. This hope may not prove well founded. For
where was the Oswald Garrison Villard of the 1950's? Who
spoke out as vociferously and courageously in the past decade on behalf of the unpopular and the unacceptable as did
Oswald Garrison Villard in the twenties?

One scholar after another had described and defended
the new American conservatism—a conservatism in which
liberty depends on concrete traditions and is menaced by
reliance on human reason, a conservatism which denies
that human beings are born naturally good and naturally
reasonable. The pragmatist and rationalist Oswald Garrison
Villard could never have understood and accepted this
point of view. Villard, who argued that all social institutions should be evaluated in terms of their practical consequences for democratic ideals and that institutions should
be modified to meet changing conditions, could never have
been persuaded to accept the thesis that freedom depends on
traditions. Villard, to whom the rationalism of man was
the very basis of his right to and potential for self-
government and liberty, to whom the rationality of mankind was the condition which would make peaceful co-
existence of nations possible, would have been appalled at
any categorical denial of man's natural reason.

Villard, who fought for the extension of democratic
political institutions and sought to breathe new life into
those already in existence at a time when economic power
threatened the democratic process in the United States,

would cry out against the words of conservative Russell Kirk:

> Very generally speaking, my point of view is that any society must have leaders; and if we do not recognize or allow an aristocracy, then we shall have an oligarchy. An aristocracy is not necessarily "feudal," though property in land is one of the best supports of true aristocracy. In any nation, the people who believe in the Republic must do their best to form a high and responsible leadership from what materials that nation has at hand. So far as men of business form a great element in our society, we need to give them responsibility and teach them responsibility; . . . a man is seldom more innocently occupied than when he is engaged in making money.[1]

Surely Oswald Garrison Villard, who more than once challenged the practice of unquestioning obedience to the state, would have welcomed a return to his alma mater to reply to that president of the Harvard New Conservative Club whose views may well reflect a tendency on the part of conservatives, eager for order and stability, to acquiesce in governmental authority and mere constitutional forms:

> What is it that the Harvard New Conservative believes? He believes, first of all, that the mind and heart of man dwells within the framework of Divine Law. He believes that society owes the individual the safeguarding

[1] Russell Kirk in a letter to the editor, *Reporter*, XIII (August 11, 1955), 7–8.

of certain rights, which are best preserved by firm limitations upon governmental authority. He believes that the individual, in return, owes society certain duties, best performed by respect for properly constituted authority. Then, he believes that among the chief means of regulating the balance between society and the individual is a judicial system, the forms and decisions of which are scrupulously observed.[2]

Surely Villard, believing in the necessity of collective social action to meet social needs, would find little comfort in reliance on a divine law and order, in a belief in the providential or invisible hand that characterizes much of the new conservatism.

Oswald Garrison Villard recognized that liberal democracy requires as great an adherence to liberalism as it does to democracy itself and that liberalism provides the objective of freedom and the faith in man which are, after all, the bases of democracy. Villard realized that a loss of faith in the common man is a threat to democracy itself, and he would have interpreted recent American conservatism as containing such a threat.

Professor Stuart Gerry Brown had assured us that a new American conservatism has indeed been abroad in the land. "If any sense can be made out of the intellectual confusion which has characterized America in the decade since the end of the Second World War," he wrote, "it would seem to be a gradually concerted movement backward—a revival of conservatism, even at times of reaction." [3] Professor

[2] William C. Brady in a letter to the editor, *Reporter*, XIII (August 11, 1955), 8.

[3] Stuart Gerry Brown, "Democracy, the New Conservatism,

Clinton Rossiter pointed to evidences of the presence of a new conservatism. He observed

> the decline in individualism and non-conformity, in hard fact if not in happy slogan; the new gains of organized religion; . . . a quickened interest in security, whether won through savings, insurance, pensions, or law; that ever-widening diffusion of property; the pervading air of nostalgia and of deep satisfaction with our institutions, and consequent distrust of the untrammeled intellect; the discrediting of the extreme Left for its flirtations with Communism; and all the pressures and irritations of life in a country threatened, as was Burke's England, by an enemy armed with ideas as well as guns.[4]

If Professors Brown and Rossiter are correct, who are these conservatives? Are they, as Richard Hofstadter suggested in a volume entitled *The New American Right*, former liberals forced to this position because "the most that the old liberals can now envisage is not to carry on with some ambitious new program, but simply to defend as much as possible of the old achievements and to try to keep traditional liberties of expression that are threatened." [5] Can it be that Professor Hofstadter was correct when he reported that "there are some signs that liberals are be-

---

and the Liberal Tradition in America," *Ethics*, LXVI (October, 1955), 1.

[4] Clinton Rossiter, "Toward an American Conservatism," *Yale Review*, XLIV (March, 1955), 354–55.

[5] Richard Hofstadter, "The Pseudo-Conservative Revolt," in Daniel Bell (ed.), *The New American Right* (New York: Criterion Books, Inc., 1955), p. 34.

ginning to find it both natural and expedient to explore the merits and employ the rhetoric of conservatism. They find themselves far more conscious of those things they would like to preserve than they are of those things they would like to change." [6] Professor Brown, in his explanation of the apparent disappearance of the New Dealers from the contemporary scene, states that

> Political thinkers who, twenty years ago, might have been speaking their pieces as bits in the liberal ferment of the New Deal, are turning nowadays to the prescriptions of Burke—and remaining largely aloof from the world of affairs. They urge upon us the ideas of eccentrics like Calhoun and John Randolph of Roanoke; they teach us that the American Revolution was in fact no revolution at all. The talk is of conservatism and of distrust in equality and democracy. [7]

Samuel Lubell, too, has commented on the new activities of the New Dealers: "At home, the New Deal generation, once so zealous to make America over, devotes its evenings to wrestling with mortgage payments and inculcating a respect for tradition and discipline in overly progressive children." [8]

If Professors Brown and Hofstadter and Lubell are correct in their conclusion that the liberals of yesterday have turned conservative, then Oswald Garrison Villard is all the more

[6] Richard Hofstadter, *The Age of Reform* (New York: Alfred A. Knopf, Inc., 1955), p. 13.

[7] Brown, *op. cit.*, p. 1.

[8] Samuel Lubell, *The Revolt of the Moderates* (New York: Harper & Bros., 1956), p. 4.

deserving of attention, for he becomes representative of the last of the outstanding figures in the history of the American liberal tradition. As such, his ideas and activities deserve recognition. As such, he played a notable and constructive part in the history of American liberalism.

Bibliographical Notes

THE PUBLISHED WRITINGS of Oswald Garrison Villard and the Villard manuscript collection in the Houghton Library of Harvard University constitute the main sources of this work. The manuscript collection consists of correspondence, unpublished speeches, and memorabilia. Of particular significance have been, of course, past volumes of the *Nation* and Villard's *Fighting Years: Memoirs of a Liberal Editor* (New York: Harcourt, Brace & Co., 1939). No other biography of Villard has yet appeared. Unless otherwise indicated by footnote, quotations attributed to Villard are from either the Villard manuscripts or Villard's writings in the *Nation*.

There are a number of histories of the twenties. One of the best and most entertaining is that of Frederick Lewis Allen, *Only Yesterday* (New York: Harper & Bros., 1931); see also Frederick J. Hoffman, *The Twenties* (New York: The Viking Press, Inc., 1955). For the political views of the *Nation*, see Alan P. Grimes, *The Political Liberalism of the New York Nation, 1865–1932* (Chapel Hill: University of North Carolina Press, 1953).

CHAPTER I

On the history of the American liberal tradition, the two volumes of Richard Hofstadter, *The American Political Tradition and the Men Who Made It* (New York: Alfred A. Knopf, Inc., 1948) and *The Age of Reform* (New York: Alfred A. Knopf, Inc., 1955) are among the best; also Eric Goldman, *Rendezvous with Destiny* (New York: Vintage Books, Inc., 1956). For a comparison of liberalism old and new, see Reinhold Niebuhr, "Liberalism: Illusions and Realities," *New Republic*, July 4, 1955, pp. 11–13. On the evolution of liberalism, Harry Girvetz, *From Wealth to Welfare* (Stanford: Stanford University Press, 1950) is invaluable.

CHAPTER II

For his own recollections of his life, see Villard's *Fighting Years*, cited above. For those of his father, see Henry Villard, *Memoirs of Henry Villard* (2 vols., Boston and New York: Houghton Mifflin Co., 1904). For background material on William Lloyd Garrison and abolitionism, Hazel Catherine Wolf, *On Freedom's Altar* (Madison: University of Wisconsin Press, 1952) and Ralph Korngold, *Two Friends of Man: The Story of William Lloyd Garrison and Wendell Phillips and Their Relationship with Abraham Lincoln* (Boston: Little, Brown & Co., 1950) are of note.

CHAPTER III

One of the finest treatments of civil liberties in this period is Zechariah Chafee, Jr., *Free Speech in the United States* (Cambridge: Harvard University Press, 1941). On selected aspects of civil liberties in the twenties, the following are valuable: Robert K. Murray, *The Red Scare* (Minneapolis: University of Minnesota Press, 1955); Louis F. Post, *The Deportations Delirium of 1920* (Chicago: Charles H. Kerr & Co., 1923); Norman Hapgood, *Professional Patriots* (New York: A. & C. Boni, Inc., 1927); Charles Merz, *The Dry Decade* (Garden City: Doubleday & Co., Inc., 1931); Felix Frankfurter, *The Case of Sacco and Vanzetti* (New York: Little, Brown & Co., 1927); *Nicola Sacco, Defendant, the Sacco-Vanzetti Case* (5 vols., New York: Henry Holt & Co., Inc., 1928–29); also about Sacco and Vanzetti is Herbert B. Ehrmann, *The Untried Case* (New York: Vanguard Press, 1933). See also McAlister Coleman, *Eugene V. Debs, A*

Man Unafraid (New York: Greenburg, 1930) and Ralph Chaplin, *Wobbly* (Chicago: University of Chicago Press, 1948). Carleton Parker, "The I.W.W.," *Atlantic Monthly*, CXX (November, 1917), is an excellent piece also.

CHAPTER IV

For Villard's role in the founding of the NAACP, see Mary White Ovington, *The Walls Came Tumbling Down* (New York: Harcourt, Brace & Co., 1947). On problems of the American Indian, see Oliver La Farge and others, *The Changing Indian* (Norman: University of Oklahoma Press, 1942); on the immigrant, both Carl F. Wittke, *We Who Built America* (New York: Prentice-Hall, Inc., 1940) and George M. Stephenson, *A History of American Immigration* (New York: Ginn and Co., 1926) are noteworthy; Oscar Handlin, *The Uprooted* (Boston: Little, Brown & Co., 1951) is scholarly and dramatic. Characteristic of the literature on American racism are Henry Pratt Fairchild, *The Melting Pot Mistake* (Boston: Little, Brown & Co., 1926); Madison Grant, *The Passing of the Great Race* (New York: Charles Scribner's Sons, 1916); Madison Grant and Charles Stewart Davison (eds.), *The Alien in Our Midst* (New York: Galton Publishing Co., 1930); and, of course, Lothrop Stoddard, *The Rising Tide of Color* (New York: Charles Scribner's Sons, 1920). For a detailed account of the labor unrest of the twenties, see Foster Rhea Dulles, *Labor in America* (New York: Thomas Y. Crowell Co., 1949); on labor's decline during the period, see Emanuel Stein and Jerome Davis (eds.), *Labor Problems in America* (New York: Farrar & Rinehart, Inc., 1940).

CHAPTER V

On the case of Victor Berger, see Chafee, *Free Speech in the United States*, cited above. On the nature of the judiciary in the period under study, see Louis B. Boudin, *Government by Judiciary* (New York: William Godwin, Inc., 1932).

CHAPTER VI

On the development of third parties during the twenties, see William B. Hesseltine, *The Rise and Fall of Third Parties* (Washington, D.C.: Public Affairs Press, 1948) and Murray S. Stedman, Jr., and Susan W. Stedman, *Discontent at the Polls: A Study of Farmer and Labor Parties, 1827–1948* (New York: Columbia University Press, 1950). Invaluable is Kenneth MacKay's *The Progressive Movement of 1924* (New York: Columbia University Press, 1947).

CHAPTER VII

On the relationship between big business and recent American liberalism, see Thomas P. Neill, *The Rise and Decline of Liberalism* (Milwaukee: The Bruce Publishing Co., 1953); Irwin Ross, *Strategy for Liberals: The Politics of the Mixed Economy* (New York: Harper & Bros., 1949); Girvetz, *From Wealth to Welfare*, cited previously; and Louis Hartz, *The Liberal Tradition in America* (New York: Harcourt, Brace & Co., 1955).

CHAPTER VIII

Among the significant works on pacifism, the following have been found useful here: Florence B. Boeckel, *Between War and Peace* (New York: The Macmillan Co., 1928); Merle Curti, *Peace or War: The American Struggle, 1636–1936* (New York: W. W. Norton & Co., Inc., 1936); Philip E. Jacob, *Conscription of Conscience* (Ithaca: Cornell University Press, 1952); and H. C. Peterson and Gilbert Fite, *Opponents of War, 1917–1918* (Madison: University of Wisconsin Press, 1957). On various phases of international relations throughout the period, the following are helpful: Raymond L. Buell, *The Washington Conference* (New York: D. Appleton & Co., 1922); Ray Stannard Baker, *Woodrow Wilson and World Settlement* (New York: Doubleday, Page and Co., 1927); James Kerney, *The Political Education of Woodrow Wilson* (New York: The Century Co., 1926); Alfred Lief, *Democracy's Norris* (New York: The Stackpole Co., 1939); Sir James O'Connor, *History of Ireland, 1798–1924* (New York: George H. Doran Co., 1926); Nicholas Mansergh, *Ireland in the Age of Reform and Revolution* (London: George Allen and Unwin, Ltd., 1940); Robert Morss Lovett, *All Our Years* (New York: The Viking Press, Inc., 1948); Chester Lloyd Jones, *The Caribbean Since 1900* (New York: Prentice-Hall, Inc., 1936); Arthur C. Millspaugh, *Haiti Under American Control, 1915–1930* (Boston: World Peace Foundation, 1931); and L. L. Montague, *Haiti and the United States, 1714–1938* (Durham, N.C.: Duke University Press, 1940).

CHAPTER IX

Of special significance among the works on the new American conservatism are the following: Daniel Bell (ed.), *The New American Right* (New York: Criterion Books, Inc., 1955); William M. Buckley, *Up from Liberalism* (New York: McDowell, Obolensky, Inc., 1959); Gordon Harrison, *Road to the Right* (New York: William Morrow & Co., Inc., 1954); Russell Kirk, *The Conservative Mind* (Chicago, 1953); Clinton Rossiter, *Conservatism in America* (New York: Alfred A. Knopf, Inc., 1955); and Peter Viereck's *Conservatism Revisited* (New York: Charles Scribner's Sons, 1949) and *The Shame and Glory of the Intellectuals* (Boston: Beacon Press, 1953).

Index

Colophon

OSWALD GARRISON VILLARD, *Liberal of the 1920's* has been set in 10 point Linotype Janson, leaded 3 points, printed on 60 pound P. H. Glatfelter antique standard white text paper, R grade, and bound in Columbia Bayside Linen over 70 point binder's board by the Vail-Ballou Press, Inc.

SU PRESS